MAST
CHA GPT
AND PROMPT
ENGINEERING

MORE THAN 120 PROMPT EXAMPLES READY TO USE

CUANTUM

UPDATED 2023

Mastering ChatGPT and Prompt Engineering

First Edition

Copyright © 2023 Cuantum Technologies

First edition: April 2023

Published by Cuantum Technologies LLC.

Dallas, TX.

ISBN 9798390306932

"AI will probably most likely lead to the
end of the world, but in the meantime,
there'll be great companies."

- Sam Altman, CEO of OpenAI

TABLE OF CONTENTS

CLAIM YOUR
FREE MONTH

As part of our reward program for our readers, we want to give you a **full free month** of...

www.cuantum.ai

THE PROCESS IS SIMPLE

1 Go to Amazon and leave us your amazing book review

2 Send us your name and date of review to books@cuantum.tech

3 Join **cuantum.ai** and we will activate the Creator Plan for you, free of charge.

What is CuantumAI?

All-in-one AI powered content generator and money factory

A complete Eco-system

AI Powerded Chatbot Mentors - Templates - Documents - Images - Audio/Text Transcriptions - And more...

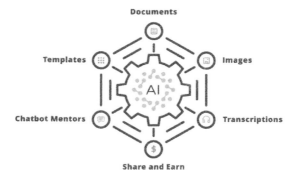

Get all your AI needs in one place to boost productivity, advance your career, or start an AI-powered business.

Do the research - Write the content - Generate the Image - Publish - Earn Money

CLAIM IT TODAY! LIMITED AVAILABILITY

Who we are

Welcome to this book created by Cuantum Technologies. We are a team of passionate developers who are committed to creating software that delivers creative experiences and solves real-world problems. Our focus is on building high-quality web applications that provide a seamless user experience and meet the needs of our clients.

At our company, we believe that programming is not just about writing code. It's about solving problems and creating solutions that make a difference in people's lives. We are constantly exploring new technologies and techniques to stay at the forefront of the industry, and we are excited to share our knowledge and experience with you through this book.

Our approach to software development is centered around collaboration and creativity. We work closely with our clients to understand their needs and create solutions that are tailored to their specific requirements. We believe that software should be intuitive, easy to use, and visually appealing, and we strive to create applications that meet these criteria.

In this book, we aim to provide you with a practical and hands-on approach to practice Python programming. Whether you are a beginner with no programming experience or an experienced programmer looking to expand your skills, this book is designed to help you develop your skills and build a solid foundation in Python programming.

Our Philosophy:

At the heart of Cuantum, we believe that the best way to create software is through collaboration and creativity. We value the input of our clients, and we work closely with them to create solutions that meet their needs. We also believe that software should be intuitive, easy to use, and visually appealing, and we strive to create applications that meet these criteria.

We also believe that programming is a skill that can be learned and developed over time. We encourage our developers to explore new technologies and techniques, and we provide them with the tools and resources they need to stay at the forefront of the industry. We also believe that programming should be fun and rewarding, and we strive to create a work environment that fosters creativity and innovation.

Our Expertise:

At our software company, we specialize in building web applications that deliver creative experiences and solve real-world problems. Our developers have expertise in a wide range of programming languages and frameworks, including Python, Django, React, Three.js, and Vue.js, among others. We are constantly exploring new technologies and techniques to stay at the forefront of the industry, and we pride ourselves on our ability to create solutions that meet our clients' needs.

We also have extensive experience in data analysis and visualization, machine learning, and artificial intelligence. We believe that these technologies have the potential to transform the way we live and work, and we are excited to be at the forefront of this revolution.

In conclusion, our company is focused on creating software web for creative experiences and solving real-world problems. We believe in collaboration and creativity, and we strive to create solutions that are intuitive, easy to use, and visually appealing. We are passionate about programming, and we are excited to share our knowledge and experience with you through this book. Whether you are a beginner or an experienced programmer, we hope that you find this book to be a valuable resource in your journey to become a proficient Python programmer.

Introduction

Welcome to **"Mastering ChatGPT and Prompt Engineering: From Beginner to Expert,"** a book designed to provide you with an in-depth understanding of prompt engineering and its various applications. As a leading software development company, Cuantum Technologies is proud to share our expertise in this rapidly evolving field with the aim of empowering individuals and organizations to leverage the potential of AI-powered language models effectively and responsibly.

Prompt engineering has emerged as a critical skill for working with AI language models like OpenAI's GPT series. These models have demonstrated an incredible capacity for understanding and generating human language, opening up a world of opportunities for businesses, researchers, and individuals alike. However, to harness their full potential, it is essential to know how to guide these models effectively using carefully designed prompts.

In this book, we will take you on a comprehensive journey through the world of prompt engineering, covering everything from the fundamentals of AI language models to advanced strategies and real-world applications. Our aim is to equip you with the knowledge and skills necessary to become a proficient prompt engineer and unlock the true power of AI language models.

Chapter 1 lays the groundwork by introducing the concept of AI language models and their underlying architectures. We will explore the development of these models, their capabilities, and their limitations, setting the stage for a deep dive into prompt engineering.

In Chapter 2, we will discuss the core principles of prompt engineering, focusing on the techniques and strategies that can be employed to guide AI language models effectively. This chapter will also introduce you to the concept of priming and the importance of context in prompt design.

Chapters 3 through 6 cover a series of advanced techniques and strategies that can be employed to optimize and refine your prompts. From exploring the role of tokens and tokenization to the iterative prompt design process, these chapters will provide you with a wealth of practical knowledge and examples to enhance your prompt engineering skills.

Chapter 7 delves into the diverse range of real-world applications and use cases for prompt engineering. From content generation and editing to sentiment analysis and text classification, this chapter showcases the transformative potential of AI language models across various industries and domains.

Recognizing the importance of ethical considerations in AI, Chapter 8 addresses the challenges of bias, discrimination, privacy, and data protection in the context of prompt engineering. The chapter emphasizes the need for responsible AI deployment, transparency, and accountability to ensure that AI-powered language models are used in a manner that respects human values and fosters fairness.

Chapter 9 looks ahead to the future of prompt engineering, examining emerging AI architectures, interdisciplinary approaches, personalization and adaptive prompts, and legal and regulatory developments. This forward-looking chapter highlights the ongoing evolution of AI and the importance of staying current with new trends and developments.

Lastly, Chapter 10 concludes the book by summarizing the key takeaways and offering guidance on continuing your prompt engineering journey. This final chapter emphasizes the symbiotic relationship between humans and AI, envisioning a future where the collaboration between the two leads to unprecedented innovation and progress.

We have designed this book to be both informative and practical, providing a solid foundation in prompt engineering while also offering numerous examples and case studies to illustrate the real-world impact of these techniques. Whether you are a seasoned AI professional or just beginning your journey in this field, we hope that

"**Mastering ChatGPT and Prompt Engineering: From Beginner to Expert**" serves as a valuable resource for your ongoing exploration of AI language models and prompt engineering.

Thank you for choosing to embark on this journey with Cuantum Technologies. We wish you the best of luck in your prompt engineering endeavors and look forward to seeing the incredible innovations that you will undoubtedly contribute to the world of AI.

Cuantum Technologies

CHAPTER 1: Introduction

Prompts are a crucial and indispensable component of working with language models like GPT-4. These models rely heavily on the input queries that prompts provide, as they guide the model's responses and enable users to leverage the power of AI to accomplish a wide range of tasks. These tasks can include anything from generating content to answering complex questions.

Moreover, prompts that are carefully crafted and thoughtfully designed can unlock the full potential of these models, making them an invaluable tool for a broad range of applications across various domains. For instance, in the field of natural language processing, well-crafted prompts can help researchers develop algorithms that can better understand and analyze human language. Similarly, in the field of education, prompts can be used to design interactive learning experiences that engage students and promote critical thinking skills.

As such, it is clear that prompts play a vital role in the effective utilization of language models. By providing the necessary guidance for these models, prompts can help users achieve their goals and accomplish tasks that would otherwise be challenging or impossible.

As developers, we want to emphasize that the ability to create effective prompts is critical to maximize the utility of AI language models. To better understand the power of prompts, let's delve into a few examples:

Example 1: Creative Writing Assistance Suppose you're an aspiring writer who wants to generate a compelling opening paragraph for a science fiction novel. Crafting the right prompt can make all the difference. A vague, uninformative prompt like "Write an opening paragraph for a book" may yield an unsatisfactory or generic response. However, a more specific and detailed prompt like "Write an intriguing opening paragraph for a science fiction novel set in a dystopian future where humans coexist with sentient robots" is more likely to produce a captivating and relevant result.

Example 2: Research Assistance Imagine you're a researcher looking to gather information on the effects of climate change on polar bear populations. A poorly formulated prompt, such as "Tell me about climate change," may result in an overly broad response that doesn't focus on your specific area of interest. On the other hand, a well-crafted prompt like "Explain the impact of climate change on polar bear populations, including factors such as habitat loss, reduced sea ice, and shifting food sources" will yield a focused and informative answer tailored to your needs.

These examples illustrate the importance of prompt engineering in unlocking the potential of AI language models. In this book, you'll learn the principles, techniques, and best practices needed to become proficient in prompt engineering. We'll cover everything from foundational concepts to advanced strategies, ensuring that by the end, you'll be well-equipped to craft effective prompts for a wide range of applications and use cases.

1.1 The Power of Prompts

The Art and Science of Prompt Engineering: Prompt engineering is both an art and a science. It requires creativity to design prompts that resonate with the intended context and elicit the desired response. Simultaneously, it demands a solid understanding of the AI model's underlying architecture and behavior, allowing you to optimize prompts for maximum efficacy. By mastering prompt engineering, you'll acquire a valuable skill set that bridges the gap between the technical and creative aspects of working with AI language models.

Enhancing Human-AI Collaboration: As AI continues to advance and permeate various aspects of our lives, the importance of effective human-AI collaboration cannot be overstated. Mastering prompt engineering empowers you to communicate with AI models more efficiently and precisely. This skill will enable you to harness AI's capabilities in a more targeted and controlled manner, resulting in a more seamless and productive collaboration.

Adapting to Future AI Developments: The landscape of AI is constantly evolving, with new models and architectures emerging regularly. As an expert in prompt engineering, you'll be better prepared to adapt to these changes and make the most of emerging AI technologies. The principles and techniques you'll learn in this book are designed to be applicable across various AI models, ensuring that your prompt engineering skills remain relevant and valuable as the field progresses.

In conclusion, the power of prompts lies in their ability to guide AI models towards generating useful, relevant, and engaging responses. By honing your prompt engineering skills, you'll unlock the full potential of AI language models, enhance human-AI collaboration, and stay at the forefront of AI developments. The following chapters will equip you with the knowledge and tools necessary to become a proficient prompt engineer, from understanding the fundamentals to mastering advanced strategies.

1.2 Importance of Prompt Engineering

The art of prompt engineering is not only vital for harnessing the full potential of AI language models, but also for ensuring that these models provide valuable, reliable, and ethical responses. In this section, we will explore the importance of prompt engineering in various aspects of AI interactions and its role in shaping the future of human-AI collaboration.

1.2.1 Improved AI Model Efficiency

Effective prompts lead to better AI performance, minimizing the need for repeated queries or extensive post-processing. As you become more proficient in crafting precise prompts, you'll be able to obtain the desired output with fewer iterations, saving time and resources.

This efficiency is especially crucial for large-scale applications and high-throughput environments.

Example: A company using AI for customer support can benefit from well-crafted prompts, enabling the AI to understand user issues and provide accurate solutions without the need for repeated clarification or excessive back-and-forth.

1.2.2 Enhanced User Experience

Creating user-friendly and intuitive prompts enhances the overall experience for individuals interacting with AI systems. An effective prompt design considers the end-user's perspective, making AI responses more accessible, informative, and engaging.

Example: An AI-powered chatbot that can understand and respond to natural language queries, thanks to well-designed prompts, can make the user experience more seamless and enjoyable compared to a system that requires rigid, structured inputs.

1.2.3 Addressing AI Bias and Fairness

Prompt engineering plays a crucial role in mitigating AI biases and ensuring fairness in model responses. By carefully crafting prompts that consider potential pitfalls, biases, and ethical concerns, you can help guide AI systems to generate more balanced and fair responses.

Example: When creating prompts for a job description generator, considering potential gender or cultural biases can lead to more inclusive and unbiased job descriptions, thus contributing to a fairer hiring process.

1.2.4 Customization and Adaptability

Mastering prompt engineering allows you to customize AI responses for specific applications or industries. By tailoring prompts to the context and requirements of a particular use case, you can ensure that AI outputs are relevant, accurate, and meaningful.

Example: A financial analyst using AI for forecasting can create prompts that focus on specific economic indicators, market trends, and timeframes to generate tailored predictions that cater to their unique needs and analysis goals.

1.2.5 Preparing for Future AI Developments

As AI models continue to evolve and become more sophisticated, prompt engineering will remain a key skill for optimizing AI interactions. By mastering prompt engineering, you'll be better equipped to adapt to new AI advancements and leverage these technologies to their fullest potential.

1.2.6 Fostering AI-Driven Innovation

Prompt engineering not only enhances the effectiveness of AI models in existing applications but also paves the way for innovation by enabling the discovery of novel use cases. As you hone your skills in crafting effective prompts, you can explore new ways to leverage AI capabilities, driving innovation and expanding the horizons of AI applications across various domains.

Example: A researcher skilled in prompt engineering might use AI to generate new hypotheses in their field of study, helping them explore uncharted territories and potentially contributing to groundbreaking discoveries.

1.2.7 Competitive Advantage in the AI-driven Marketplace

In an increasingly AI-driven world, mastering prompt engineering can provide a significant competitive advantage. Businesses and professionals who can effectively harness AI through well-crafted prompts will be better positioned to offer superior products, services, and solutions, setting them apart from their competitors.

Example: A marketing agency that excels in prompt engineering can create more engaging, targeted, and persuasive AI-generated content, enabling them to deliver better results for their clients and stand out in a competitive market.

1.2.8 Developing a Future-proof Skill Set

As AI continues to play a more prominent role in various aspects of life and work, the demand for prompt engineering expertise will likely grow. By investing time and effort into mastering prompt engineering, you are developing a valuable and future-proof skill set that can open up new career opportunities and enhance your professional growth.

In summary, prompt engineering is a critical component in the development of AI models and user experience. However, its importance does not stop there. Prompt engineering promotes innovation, giving organizations a competitive edge in the market. It also contributes to the development of a future-proof skill set by providing individuals with the tools and knowledge needed to keep up with the ever-changing technological landscape.

With these long-term benefits in mind, this book aims not only to equip you with the knowledge and tools necessary to excel in prompt engineering and harness the full potential of AI in your chosen field, but also to provide a holistic understanding of how prompt engineering fits into the larger picture of AI development and its impact on various industries.

1.3 Overview of the Book

In this book, "Mastering Prompt Engineering: A Comprehensive Guide to Crafting Effective AI Queries," we aim to provide you with the knowledge and tools necessary to excel in prompt engineering. Through a systematic and detailed approach, we will guide you through the entire process, starting with foundational concepts and building up to advanced strategies and real-world applications. Below is a brief overview of the topics covered in each chapter, highlighting the main objectives and key takeaways.

Chapter 2: Foundations of Prompt Engineering

This chapter lays the groundwork for understanding prompt engineering by introducing the fundamentals of language models and the GPT architecture. You'll learn about the history, evolution, and key principles of prompt design that form the basis for effective prompt engineering.

Example: We'll explain how the GPT-4 architecture processes text input and generates responses, enabling you to appreciate the underlying mechanics and constraints that inform prompt engineering best practices.

Chapter 3: Advanced Prompt Engineering Techniques

In this chapter, we delve into the core components of effective prompts, including clarity, specificity, context, and constraints. We'll discuss how to address potential biases and ensure fairness in AI-generated responses.

Example: We'll provide examples of how modifying a prompt's phrasing or adding contextual information can lead to more accurate, relevant, and unbiased responses.

Chapter 4: Real-World Applications of Prompt Engineering

Here, we explore various prompt types and techniques, such as open-ended, guided, conversational, and task-specific prompts. We'll provide practical tips and examples for each type, helping you to choose the most suitable approach for your specific use case.

Example: We'll demonstrate how to create a conversational prompt that guides an AI language model to engage in a natural, interactive dialogue while providing useful information.

Chapter 5: Iterative Prompt Design Process

This chapter outlines a systematic approach to prompt design, from setting goals and defining objectives to evaluating and analyzing model responses. We'll discuss strategies for iterating and optimizing your prompts to achieve the desired results.

Example: We'll walk you through the process of refining a prompt to improve an AI-generated response, demonstrating the importance of an iterative approach to prompt engineering.

Chapter 6: Advanced Prompt Engineering Strategies

In this chapter, we'll cover more advanced prompt engineering strategies, such as multi-step prompts, systematic prompt exploration, leveraging external knowledge sources, and combining prompts for synergy.

Example: We'll show you how to create a multi-step prompt that guides the AI model through a complex problem-solving process, resulting in a comprehensive and well-structured response.

Chapter 7: Real-world Applications and Use Cases

This chapter presents a range of real-world applications and use cases for prompt engineering, including content generation, question answering, language translation, and sentiment analysis. We'll provide practical examples and tips for each application, demonstrating the versatility and value of prompt engineering across various domains.

Example: We'll demonstrate how to craft an effective prompt for sentiment analysis, enabling an AI model to accurately classify text according to its emotional tone or subjective content.

Chapter 8: Ethical Considerations in Prompt Engineering

In this chapter, we'll discuss the ethical aspects of prompt engineering, including addressing bias, privacy, transparency, and accountability. We'll provide guidance on how to approach ethical concerns and develop responsible AI deployment practices.

Example: We'll explore potential pitfalls and challenges associated with using AI-generated content in journalism, discussing how to ensure transparency and maintain ethical standards.

Chapter 9: Future Trends and Challenges

Here, we'll examine the future trends and challenges in prompt engineering, covering emerging AI architectures, personalization, interdisciplinary approaches, and legal and regulatory developments.

Example:

We'll discuss the implications of AI personalization in prompt engineering, exploring how adaptive prompts can cater to individual user needs while maintaining ethical boundaries and respecting user privacy.

By the end of this book, you will have a comprehensive understanding of prompt engineering. We will begin by exploring the fundamentals of prompt engineering, including the most effective ways to design prompts for AI language models. We will delve into advanced strategies and techniques, such as optimizing prompts for specific use cases and domains, and fine-tuning models to achieve maximum performance. Additionally, we will provide you with numerous examples and practical tips to help you apply your newfound knowledge to real-world scenarios. With this knowledge, you will be equipped with the tools and confidence needed to excel in prompt engineering and effectively utilize AI language models across a wide range of industries and applications.

CHAPTER 2: Foundations of Prompt Engineering

2.1 Language Models and GPT Architecture

Before diving into the intricacies of prompt engineering, it's essential to understand the fundamentals of language models and the GPT architecture. This knowledge will provide you with the necessary context to craft effective prompts that align with the underlying mechanics of AI language models.

2.1.1 Language Models: An Overview

Language models are computational algorithms that predict or generate sequences of words based on a given input. These models learn from large datasets of text, capturing statistical patterns in language to generate coherent and contextually relevant responses.

Example: Given the input "The weather is nice today. Let's go for a", the language model might predict "walk" or "picnic" as the next word, based on the statistical patterns it has learned from the training data.

2.1.2 Transformer Architectures

Transformer architectures form the foundation of many modern AI language models, including the GPT series. Introduced by Vaswani et al. in 2017, the Transformer architecture revolutionized natural language processing (NLP) by utilizing self-attention mechanisms and positional encoding to process text in a more efficient and context-aware manner.

Example: The self-attention mechanism allows the Transformer model to weigh the importance of each word in a sentence relative to the others, enabling it to generate more contextually accurate responses.

2.1.3 GPT: Generative Pre-trained Transformer

The GPT (Generative Pre-trained Transformer) series of language models, developed by OpenAI, are built upon the Transformer architecture. GPT models are pre-trained on massive datasets and fine-tuned for specific tasks or applications. They are particularly well-suited for tasks that involve generating human-like text, such as content creation, question-answering, and conversation.

Example: GPT-3, a predecessor to GPT-4, has 175 billion parameters, allowing it to generate highly coherent and contextually accurate text based on a given prompt.

2.1.4 How GPT Models Process Input and Generate Output

GPT models utilize a token-based approach to process input text. They segment text into tokens, which represent words or subword units, and process these tokens in parallel using self-attention mechanisms. Based on the input tokens and the learned statistical patterns, GPT models generate a probability distribution over the vocabulary for the next token, selecting the most likely token as the output.

Example: Given the input "What is the capital of France?", the GPT model processes the tokens and generates a response, such as "The capital of France is Paris."

2.1.5 Token Length and Limitations

When working with GPT models, it's essential to consider token length and limitations. Since GPT models process input text in tokens, both the input and output tokens contribute to the total token count, which is subject to the model's maximum token limit. Exceeding this limit can result in incomplete or truncated responses, which may impact the effectiveness of your prompts.

Example: Suppose the GPT model you're working with has a maximum token limit of 2048. If your input prompt has 100 tokens and the model generates a response of 1950 tokens, the total token count would be 2050, exceeding the limit. In this case, the output may be truncated, potentially affecting the quality or coherence of the response.

2.1.6 Impact of GPT Architecture Advancements on Prompt Engineering

As GPT architecture continues to advance, the models become more powerful, capable of generating more accurate and coherent text. These advancements can directly impact prompt engineering, making it even more crucial to develop effective and well-crafted prompts to harness the full potential of these increasingly sophisticated AI language models.

Example: The transition from GPT-3 to GPT-4 saw improvements in various aspects of language generation, including better context understanding and reduced biases. With these advancements, prompt engineering techniques need to evolve and adapt to ensure optimal results and maintain ethical AI practices.

In conclusion, it is important to have a thorough understanding of the basics of language models and the architecture of the GPT in order to master prompt engineering. Building on this knowledge, one must also consider the inherent limitations of these models, such as token length and computational power, and how to work within them in order to make the most effective prompts.

Additionally, it is crucial to stay up-to-date with the latest advancements in GPT technology in order to continue to improve your prompt engineering skills. By taking all of these factors into account and continually refining your approach to prompt engineering, you can create prompts that effectively leverage the strengths of GPT models while minimizing potential drawbacks.

2.2 Principles of Prompt Design

Effective prompt engineering requires an understanding of the underlying principles of prompt design. In this section, we will discuss the key principles that inform best practices in crafting prompts, enabling you to create prompts that elicit accurate, relevant, and contextually appropriate responses from AI language models.

2.2.1 Clarity and Specificity

Clear and specific prompts are more likely to yield precise and accurate responses from AI language models. By providing enough context and explicitly stating your requirements, you can guide the model towards generating the desired output.

Example: Instead of prompting with "Tell me about solar energy," use a more specific prompt like "Explain the process of converting sunlight into electricity using photovoltaic solar panels."

2.2.2 Open-ended vs. Closed-ended Questions

The type of question you ask can significantly impact the AI-generated response. Open-ended questions encourage more expansive and creative responses, while closed-ended questions typically yield concise and specific answers.

Example: Open-ended: "What are some potential benefits of electric cars?" Closed-ended: "Do electric cars produce fewer emissions than gasoline-powered cars?"

2.2.3 Using Constraints and InstructGPT

Including constraints or explicit instructions in your prompt can help guide the AI model towards generating more targeted and relevant responses. InstructGPT, an extension of GPT models, is specifically designed to follow instructions embedded within prompts.

Example: Instead of prompting with "Write an article about the benefits of exercise," you can add constraints like "Write a 500-word article about the top 5 benefits of regular aerobic exercise for mental health."

2.2.4 Managing AI-generated Content Length

To control the length of AI-generated content, you can include explicit instructions specifying the desired length or use the model's parameters, such as temperature and max tokens, to influence the output.

Example: Length instruction: "Summarize the main points of the article in 3-4 sentences." Model parameters: Set **max_tokens** to limit the number of tokens generated, or adjust **temperature** to control the randomness of the output.

2.2.5 Prompt Iteration and Refinement

Iterative prompt design is crucial for achieving optimal results. By analyzing AI-generated responses and refining your prompts, you can improve the quality and relevance of the output.

Example: Original prompt: "Give me tips on time management." Refined prompt: "Provide five practical time management techniques that can help college students balance their academic and social lives."

2.2.6 Handling Potential Biases

AI language models learn from vast amounts of text data, which may contain biases present in the training data. It's essential to be mindful of potential biases and to craft prompts that minimize or counteract these biases in the generated output.

Example: Biased prompt: "Why are women less successful in the tech industry?" Unbiased prompt: "Discuss the factors that contribute to the underrepresentation of women in the tech industry and potential strategies to address this issue."

2.2.7 Leveraging Examples within Prompts

In some cases, providing examples within your prompt can help guide the AI model towards generating more accurate and relevant responses. This technique is particularly useful when dealing with abstract or complex concepts that the model might not fully understand without additional context.

Example: Without examples: "Explain the difference between natural and artificial sources of light." With examples: "Explain the difference between natural sources of light, such as sunlight, and artificial sources of light, like LED bulbs."

By incorporating these additional principles into your prompt design, you can further enhance the effectiveness of your prompts, leading to more accurate, relevant, and unbiased AI-generated content.

One way to incorporate these principles is to focus on the concept of diversity. Diversity in prompt design means that you should strive to create prompts that are representative of different groups and viewpoints. This can be achieved by using a variety of sources for your prompts, such as news articles, social media posts, and scientific papers. Additionally, you should consider the use of inclusive language in your prompts to ensure that they are accessible to a wide range of people.

Another important principle to consider is the concept of context. Context refers to the circumstances or environment surrounding a particular prompt. By taking into account the context of a prompt, you can ensure that it is relevant and appropriate for the situation in which it will be used. For example, if you are designing prompts for a medical chatbot, you should consider the medical context in which the prompts will be used.

In combination with the other principles covered in this section, such as simplicity and clarity, these guidelines will help you build a strong foundation for mastering prompt engineering and harnessing the full potential of AI language models. By following these guidelines, you can create prompts that are not only effective and accurate, but also inclusive and contextually relevant.

2.3 Prompt Types and Techniques

In this section, we will explore various prompt types and techniques that can be employed to achieve specific outcomes when working with AI language models. Understanding these different approaches will enable you to select and apply the most suitable technique for your unique use case.

2.3.1 Information Retrieval Prompts

Information retrieval prompts are designed to extract specific pieces of information from the AI model's knowledge base.

Example: Prompt: "What is the boiling point of water at sea level in degrees Celsius?" Expected response: "The boiling point of water at sea level is 100 degrees Celsius."

2.3.2 Creative Writing Prompts

Creative writing prompts encourage the AI model to generate imaginative content, such as stories, poetry, or fictional scenarios.

Example: Prompt: "Write a short science fiction story about a time-traveling astronaut who accidentally changes the course of history." Expected response: [An original short story involving a time-traveling astronaut]

2.3.3 Instruction-based Prompts

Instruction-based prompts provide explicit directions for the AI model to follow when generating a response, often leveraging InstructGPT's capabilities.

Example: Prompt: "Translate the following English sentence into French: 'The quick brown fox jumps over the lazy dog.'" Expected response: "Le rapide renard brun saute par-dessus le chien paresseux."

2.3.4 Opinion and Perspective Prompts

Opinion and perspective prompts elicit AI-generated opinions or perspectives on a given topic or issue, often by asking the model to assume a specific role or point of view.

Example: Prompt: "As an environmentalist, what are your thoughts on the impact of plastic waste on ocean ecosystems?" Expected response: [A response that reflects an environmentalist's perspective on plastic waste and ocean ecosystems]

2.3.5 Comparative and Contrast Prompts

Comparative and contrast prompts request the AI model to analyze similarities and differences between two or more subjects, concepts, or ideas.

Example: Prompt: "Compare and contrast the advantages and disadvantages of solar energy versus wind energy as renewable energy sources." Expected response: [A response that outlines the pros and cons of solar and wind energy, highlighting the differences and similarities between the two]

2.3.6 Step-by-step Explanation Prompts

Step-by-step explanation prompts require the AI model to provide a detailed, sequential explanation of a process, method, or concept.

Example: Prompt: "Explain the process of photosynthesis in plants, step by step." Expected response: [A response that outlines the steps involved in photosynthesis]

2.3.7 Question-Answering Prompts

Question-answering prompts are designed to elicit direct and specific answers to questions, utilizing the AI model's knowledge base and reasoning capabilities.

Example: Prompt: "Who was the first person to walk on the moon?" Expected response: "Neil Armstrong was the first person to walk on the moon."

2.3.8 Multiple-Choice Prompts

Multiple-choice prompts present the AI model with a list of options and ask it to select the most appropriate or accurate answer. This prompt type can be useful for assessment, evaluation, or to guide the model towards a specific response.

Example: Prompt: "Which of the following elements is a noble gas: a) Hydrogen, b) Oxygen, c) Helium, d) Nitrogen? Choose the correct option and explain your choice." Expected response: "c) Helium is a noble gas because it has a full set of electrons in its outer shell, making it stable and chemically inert."

By incorporating these additional prompt types and techniques into your repertoire, you can not only enhance your ability to harness the power of AI language models for a wide range of applications and use cases, but also improve the quality of the outputs generated by these models. By implementing a more varied and nuanced approach to crafting prompts, you can more effectively guide the models towards producing outputs that are tailored to your specific needs and preferences.

Moreover, by continuously experimenting with new techniques and approaches, you can stay ahead of the curve and remain at the forefront of the rapidly evolving field of AI-driven language generation. With a solid understanding of these diverse approaches and a willingness to explore new territory, you'll be well-equipped to unleash the full potential of AI language models and achieve your goals and objectives with ease and confidence.

2.4 The Iterative Prompt Design Process

To achieve the best possible results with AI language models, it's essential to approach prompt engineering as an iterative process. This process involves crafting prompts, evaluating the AI-generated responses, and refining the prompts based on the observed outcomes. In this section, we will explore the key steps involved in the iterative prompt design process.

2.4.1 Drafting the Initial Prompt

Start by creating an initial prompt that aligns with your specific use case and incorporates the principles of prompt design discussed earlier. Ensure that your prompt is clear, specific, and provides sufficient context for the AI model to generate a relevant response.

Example: Initial prompt: "Write a brief summary of the main events that took place during World War II."

2.4.2 Evaluating AI-generated Responses

Once you've crafted your initial prompt, submit it to the AI model and analyze the generated response. Assess the response's accuracy, relevance, coherence, and any potential biases. Take note of any areas where the response falls short of your expectations or requirements.

Example: AI-generated response: [A brief summary of World War II events, but lacking in detail or clarity]

2.4.3 Identifying Areas for Improvement

Based on your evaluation of the AI-generated response, identify specific aspects of the prompt that could be improved or refined. Consider whether additional context, constraints, or instructions might be necessary to guide the AI model towards a more accurate and relevant response.

Example: Areas for improvement: More detailed information on key events and their significance

2.4.4 Refining the Prompt

Modify your prompt to address the identified areas for improvement, incorporating any necessary changes to context, constraints, or instructions. Ensure that your revised prompt remains clear, specific, and adheres to the principles of prompt design.

Example: Refined prompt: "Write a detailed summary of the main events that took place during World War II, focusing on their significance and impact on the global political landscape."

2.4.5 Repeating the Iterative Process

Submit your refined prompt to the AI model and evaluate the new response. Continue iterating on your prompt until the AI-generated content meets your expectations and requirements.

Example: AI-generated response: [An improved, detailed summary of World War II events, highlighting their significance and impact]

2.4.6 Testing Prompts Across Scenarios

To ensure the effectiveness of your prompts, test them across a range of scenarios, domains, and use cases. This will help you identify any potential shortcomings or areas for improvement that may be specific to certain contexts or situations.

Example: Test your refined World War II summary prompt with other historical events, such as the American Civil War, to assess the prompt's effectiveness in generating accurate and relevant summaries across different historical contexts.

2.4.7 Incorporating Feedback from Users or Subject Matter Experts

When refining your prompts, consider incorporating feedback from users or subject matter experts who have knowledge of the specific domain or use case. Their insights can help you identify potential areas for improvement and ensure that your prompts are well-suited to the intended application.

Example: Share the AI-generated World War II summary with a history teacher or historian and solicit their feedback on the accuracy, relevance, and clarity of the content. Use their feedback to further refine your prompt as needed.

By incorporating these additional steps into the iterative prompt design process, you can further enhance the effectiveness of your prompts and ensure that they perform optimally across a wide range of scenarios, domains, and use cases. One way to do this is to conduct extensive usability testing and gather feedback from a diverse group of users. This feedback can then be used to refine and improve the prompts, making them more suited to the needs and preferences of different users.

Another key aspect of prompt engineering is to consider the context in which the prompts will be used. This includes taking into account factors such as the user's location, the time of day, and the device they are using. By tailoring prompts to these contextual factors, you can provide a more personalized and intuitive user experience.

Furthermore, it is important to continuously test, refine, and incorporate feedback into your prompt engineering practice. This iterative approach ensures that your prompts evolve over time to better meet the needs of users and perform optimally across a variety of scenarios and use cases. By implementing these best practices, you will be better equipped to create prompts that yield accurate, relevant, and contextually appropriate responses from AI language models.

CHAPTER 3: Advanced Prompt Engineering Techniques

3.1 Leveraging Model Parameters and Settings

In addition to refining prompts, you can also optimize AI-generated content by adjusting model parameters and settings. This section will discuss key parameters that influence the behavior of AI language models and how to fine-tune these settings to achieve desired results.

3.1.1 Temperature

Temperature is a parameter that controls the randomness of the AI model's output. Higher temperatures (e.g., 1.0) result in more random and creative responses, while lower temperatures (e.g., 0.1) produce more focused and deterministic responses.

Example: For a creative writing prompt, you might set the temperature to 1.0 to encourage more imaginative responses. Conversely, for a fact-based question, you might set the temperature to 0.1 to generate more precise answers.

3.1.2 Max Tokens

The **max_tokens** parameter determines the maximum number of tokens (words or word pieces) the AI model can generate in response to a prompt. By adjusting this parameter, you can control the length of the generated content.

Example: To limit the response to a 280-character tweet, you can set the **max_tokens** parameter to a value that corresponds to the desired character count.

3.1.3 Top-k Sampling

Top-k sampling is a technique that selects the AI model's output from the top k most likely tokens. Adjusting the value of k can influence the diversity and quality of the generated content.

Example: For a more focused and relevant output, you might set k to a lower value, such as 10. For a more diverse and creative output, you might set k to a higher value, like 50.

3.1.4 Top-p Sampling (Nucleus Sampling)

Top-p sampling, also known as nucleus sampling, selects tokens from the smallest set of tokens whose cumulative probability exceeds a given threshold p. This approach balances the trade-off between creativity and focus in the generated output.

Example: For a more focused output, you might set p to a lower value, such as 0.7. For a more creative output, you might set p to a higher value, like 0.9.

3.1.5 Prompt Chaining

Prompt chaining is a technique that involves breaking down a complex task into a series of simpler, related prompts. By guiding the AI model through these prompts sequentially, you can generate more coherent and accurate responses for complex or multi-step problems.

Example: Suppose you want the AI model to provide a summary of a scientific paper, followed by an analysis of its strengths and weaknesses. Instead of asking for both components in a single prompt, you can break the task into two prompts:

1. **First prompt**: "Summarize the main findings and conclusions of the following scientific paper: [paper title and abstract]." AI-generated response: [Summary of the paper]
2. **Second prompt**: "Based on the summary provided, analyze the strengths and weaknesses of the paper's methodology and conclusions." AI-generated response: [Analysis of the paper's strengths and weaknesses]

By incorporating prompt chaining into your prompt engineering practice, you can take your AI model to the next level. Prompt chaining is a technique that involves structuring the prompts in such a way that the model can understand the context of the conversation and generate more coherent and accurate responses. Essentially, it involves creating a chain of prompts that build on each other to gradually guide the model towards a more precise understanding of the user's intent.

This technique is particularly useful for tackling complex tasks, as it helps the model break down the task into smaller, more manageable pieces. For example, if you were building a chatbot to help customers troubleshoot technical issues with a product, you could use prompt chaining to guide the conversation from an initial greeting to a series of more specific prompts about the customer's problem. This would allow the model to understand the problem in greater detail and provide more accurate and relevant suggestions for how to solve it.

Of course, prompt chaining is just one of many advanced techniques and model parameters that can be used to enhance the performance of AI language models. However, when used in combination with these other techniques, it can help you unlock the full potential of these models for a wide range of applications and use cases. Whether you're building a chatbot, a virtual assistant, or any other type of conversational AI system, prompt chaining is a powerful tool that can help you take your model to the next level and provide a more engaging and satisfying user experience.

3.2 Bias Mitigation and Ethical Considerations

As you work with AI language models, it's crucial to consider the ethical implications and potential biases present in the generated content. In this section, we will discuss strategies for identifying and mitigating biases, as well as best practices for using AI models responsibly.

3.2.1 Identifying Biases

AI language models learn from vast amounts of text data, which may contain biases present in the training data. To identify these biases, analyze the AI-generated content for any potential stereotypes, inaccuracies, or skewed perspectives.

Example: If the AI model generates a response that portrays a specific gender, race, or profession in a stereotypical or biased manner, it may be indicative of biases present in the model.

3.2.2 Mitigating Biases

To mitigate biases in AI-generated content, refine your prompts to encourage the model to produce more balanced, accurate, and inclusive responses. You can also adjust model parameters and settings to influence the generated content.

Example: If the AI model produces a biased response, you can modify the prompt to explicitly request an unbiased perspective, such as: "Provide an unbiased analysis of the impact of [topic] on different genders, races, and socioeconomic groups."

3.2.3 Responsible AI Use

When using AI language models, it's important to adhere to ethical guidelines and best practices. Be transparent about the use of AI-generated content, consider the potential consequences of the generated output, and ensure that your applications align with the principles of fairness, accountability, and transparency.

Example: If you're using AI-generated content for a news article, clearly indicate that the content was generated by an AI model to avoid misleading readers. Additionally, review the content for accuracy and potential biases before publishing.

3.2.4 Evaluating AI-generated Content

To ensure the quality and ethical use of AI-generated content, establish a process for evaluating and reviewing the generated output. This should involve assessing the content for accuracy, relevance, biases, and any other factors that may impact the integrity of the content.

Example: Create a checklist or set of guidelines for evaluating AI-generated content, considering factors such as accuracy, clarity, coherence, biases, and ethical implications. Share these guidelines with team members who review and approve AI-generated content.

3.2.5 Promoting Transparency

Promote transparency by clearly communicating when content is AI-generated and educating users about the capabilities and limitations of AI language models. This can help manage expectations and foster trust in AI-generated content.

Example: If your organization uses AI-generated content on a website or blog, include a clear statement or disclosure that the content was generated by an AI language model. Consider providing additional information about the AI model's capabilities, limitations, and the steps taken to ensure the quality and accuracy of the content.

By integrating evaluation and transparency practices into your prompt engineering process, you can further enhance the quality, trustworthiness, and responsible use of AI-generated content. These practices not only contribute to the ethical use of AI language models but also help ensure that the generated content meets the highest standards of accuracy, relevance, and inclusivity.

One way to integrate evaluation into your prompt engineering process is to gather feedback from a diverse group of users who can provide insight into the content's relevance and inclusivity. By incorporating this feedback into your prompt engineering process, you can be confident that the AI-generated content is meeting the needs of a wider audience.

Transparency is also essential in ensuring the responsible use of AI-generated content. By making the prompt engineering process transparent and providing information on how the AI model is trained and the data it uses, users can have a better understanding of the content they are consuming. This transparency can also help address concerns around bias and misinformation that may arise from AI-generated content.

Overall, the integration of evaluation and transparency practices can help improve the quality and ethical use of AI-generated content. By prioritizing these practices, content creators can be confident that their AI-generated content is meeting the highest standards of accuracy, relevance, and inclusivity while also being responsible and transparent.

3.3 Collaborative Prompt Engineering

Collaborative prompt engineering involves working with other experts, team members, or stakeholders to refine and optimize prompts. This collaborative approach can enhance the effectiveness of prompts by incorporating diverse perspectives and expertise. In this section, we will discuss strategies for effective collaboration in prompt engineering.

3.3.1 Soliciting Input from Experts

When designing prompts for specific domains or use cases, consult with subject matter experts to ensure the prompts are accurate, relevant, and well-suited to the intended application. Experts can provide valuable insights and suggestions to improve the prompts.

Example: If you're creating prompts for a medical application, collaborate with healthcare professionals or medical researchers to ensure your prompts are accurate, relevant, and adhere to industry standards and best practices.

3.3.2 Engaging Team Members

Engage team members from different backgrounds, expertise, and perspectives in the prompt engineering process. This can help identify potential issues, biases, or areas for improvement that may not be apparent to a single individual.

Example: Organize regular brainstorming sessions or prompt review meetings with team members to collaboratively refine and optimize prompts. Encourage open communication and constructive feedback to facilitate continuous improvement.

3.3.3 Iterative Feedback Loops

Establish iterative feedback loops with stakeholders or end-users to continuously refine and improve your prompts. This process involves gathering feedback, incorporating it into your prompt design, and retesting the prompts to assess their effectiveness.

Example: Create a feedback form or survey for end-users to provide input on AI-generated content. Use this feedback to identify areas for improvement and refine your prompts accordingly. Periodically retest the prompts and gather additional feedback to ensure continuous improvement.

3.3.4 Documenting Best Practices

Document best practices, guidelines, and lessons learned from your collaborative prompt engineering efforts. This can help establish a shared understanding of effective prompt design principles and facilitate more efficient and effective collaboration.

Example: Create a shared knowledge base or wiki with guidelines, tips, and examples of effective prompts. Encourage team members and collaborators to contribute their insights and experiences to the knowledge base for continuous learning and improvement.

3.3.5 Establishing a Prompt Repository

A prompt repository is a centralized collection of prompts that have been tested, refined, and optimized for various domains and use cases. By establishing a prompt repository, you can streamline the prompt engineering process and facilitate knowledge sharing among collaborators.

Example: Create a shared database or platform where team members and collaborators can access, contribute, and update a collection of prompts. This repository can be organized by domain, use case, or other relevant categories to make it easy for users to find and use the most effective prompts for their specific needs.

Encourage team members and collaborators to contribute new prompts, as well as to refine and optimize existing prompts based on their experiences and expertise. By maintaining an up-to-date prompt repository, your team can ensure that they are leveraging the most effective prompts for their projects and benefiting from the collective knowledge and experience of the group.

Incorporating a prompt repository into your collaborative prompt engineering practice can help optimize the efficiency and effectiveness of your prompt design efforts. This centralized resource not only facilitates knowledge sharing and collaboration but also ensures that your team has access to the best possible prompts for their specific domains and use cases.

3.4 Evaluation Metrics and Fine-Tuning

In order to optimize your prompt engineering efforts, it's essential to evaluate the performance of AI-generated content and fine-tune your prompts and model parameters accordingly. In this section, we will discuss various evaluation metrics and fine-tuning techniques that can be used to enhance the effectiveness of your prompt engineering.

3.4.1 Evaluation Metrics

When assessing the performance of AI-generated content, consider both qualitative and quantitative evaluation metrics. These can include accuracy, relevance, coherence, fluency, and adherence to the prompt's instructions. You can also track user engagement metrics, such as click-through rates, conversions, or shares, to gauge the effectiveness of the content in achieving its intended goals.

Example: Develop a scoring rubric that evaluates AI-generated content based on factors such as accuracy, coherence, fluency, and adherence to the prompt. Use this rubric to assess the content's performance and identify areas for improvement.

3.4.2 Fine-Tuning Prompts

Based on your evaluation results, fine-tune your prompts by adjusting the wording, structure, or context to better guide the AI model. This can involve adding more specific instructions, removing ambiguity, or including additional context to enhance the quality and relevance of the generated content.

Example: If an AI-generated article is lacking in depth or detail, you can refine the prompt by adding specific questions or topics that the content should address, such as: "Discuss the pros and cons of each approach, providing real-world examples and case studies to support your analysis."

3.4.3 Fine-Tuning Model Parameters

In addition to refining your prompts, you can also adjust the model's parameters to influence the generated content. This can include adjusting temperature, token length, or other model-specific settings to optimize the content's coherence, creativity, or relevance.

Example: If the AI-generated content is too conservative or repetitive, you can increase the temperature parameter to encourage the model to generate more creative and diverse responses.

3.4.4 Iterative Optimization

Use an iterative approach to optimize your prompt engineering efforts, continuously evaluating the AI-generated content and fine-tuning your prompts and model parameters based on the results. This iterative process allows you to progressively improve the performance of the AI model, ensuring that it meets the desired objectives and quality standards.

Example: Establish a regular schedule for reviewing AI-generated content, fine-tuning prompts and model parameters, and retesting the performance of the AI model. By iteratively refining your prompt engineering process, you can continuously improve the quality and effectiveness of the generated content.

3.4.5 Benchmarking and Comparing AI Models

In some cases, you may want to compare the performance of different AI models or versions to determine which one best meets your needs. By benchmarking and comparing models based on standardized evaluation metrics, you can make informed decisions about which model to use for your specific prompt engineering tasks.

Example: Create a set of test prompts that cover a range of topics and domains relevant to your use case. Use these prompts to generate content with different AI models or versions, and assess the generated content based on your evaluation metrics. Compare the results to determine which model best meets your requirements in terms of quality, relevance, and other factors.

Benchmarking and comparing AI models can help you make informed decisions about which model to use for your prompt engineering tasks. This is important because there are many AI models available, and they vary in their effectiveness and suitability for different needs.

With benchmarking and comparison, you can evaluate multiple models and determine which one works best for your specific task.

Incorporating benchmarking and comparison into your evaluation and fine-tuning process can also help you optimize the performance of your AI-generated content. By comparing the output of different models, you can identify areas for improvement and adjust your approach accordingly. This can lead to more accurate and relevant content that better meets the needs of your audience.

Overall, benchmarking and comparing AI models is a valuable tool for anyone involved in prompt engineering. By taking the time to evaluate and compare different models, you can ensure that you are using the most effective and suitable AI language model for your specific needs. This can lead to better performance, more accurate content, and ultimately, greater success in your prompt engineering efforts.

CHAPTER 4: Real-World Applications of Prompt Engineering

4.1 Content Generation and Marketing

Effective prompt engineering can be invaluable in content generation and marketing applications, where AI-generated content can supplement or streamline the content creation process. In this section, we will discuss various applications of prompt engineering in the context of content generation and marketing.

4.1.1 Blog Posts and Articles

AI language models can be used to draft blog posts and articles on a variety of topics. By crafting well-structured prompts, you can guide the AI model to generate coherent, relevant, and engaging content that aligns with your desired tone, style, and messaging.

Example: If you need a blog post on the benefits of solar energy, you can use a prompt like: "Write a 1,000-word blog post discussing the top 5 benefits of solar energy for homeowners, focusing on environmental impact, cost savings, and long-term investment potential."

4.1.2 Social Media Content

Prompt engineering can be used to generate social media content, including tweets, Instagram captions, Facebook posts, and LinkedIn updates. By tailoring your prompts to the specific platform and audience, you can create engaging and shareable content that resonates with your target audience.

Example: To generate a tweet promoting an upcoming event, you can use a prompt like: "Write a tweet announcing the [event name], highlighting its key features and benefits, and encouraging followers to register using the provided link."

4.1.3 Email Campaigns

AI-generated content can be used to create email campaigns, newsletters, and promotional materials. By designing prompts that focus on specific goals, such as driving engagement, increasing open rates, or promoting a product or service, you can generate effective email content that resonates with your audience.

Example: To create a promotional email for a new product, you can use a prompt like: "Write a 300-word promotional email introducing the [product name], explaining its key features and benefits, and offering a limited-time discount code to encourage immediate purchases."

4.1.4 Product Descriptions

Prompt engineering can be used to create product descriptions for e-commerce websites, catalogs, and marketing materials. By crafting prompts that emphasize the unique selling points and benefits of a product, you can generate compelling descriptions that encourage potential customers to make a purchase.

Example: To generate a product description for a new laptop, you can use a prompt like: "Write a 200-word product description for the [laptop model], focusing on its sleek design, powerful performance, and innovative features that make it an ideal choice for professionals and creatives alike."

4.1.5 Idea Generation and Brainstorming

Prompt engineering can be used to facilitate idea generation and brainstorming, helping you come up with new content ideas, marketing strategies, or campaign concepts. By crafting prompts that encourage the AI model to think creatively and explore various possibilities, you can generate a diverse range of ideas and insights to inspire your content and marketing efforts.

Example: To generate ideas for blog post topics in the technology industry, you can use a prompt like: "List 20 unique and engaging blog post ideas focusing on the latest trends, innovations, and challenges in the technology industry. Each idea should include a potential title and a brief description of the content."

By leveraging prompt engineering in idea generation and brainstorming, you can harness the creative potential of AI language models to inspire and enhance your content and marketing efforts.

Prompt engineering involves creating specific prompts or questions tailored to your business or industry, which can then be used to generate new and unique ideas using AI language models. This process can help you come up with a wider range of ideas than you might be able to on your own, and can also help you identify new trends and areas of interest for your target audience.

In addition to helping you generate new ideas, AI language models can also help you enhance your existing content. By using these models to analyze your past content and identify patterns and themes, you can gain insights into what resonates with your audience and use this information to create more effective content in the future.

Overall, leveraging prompt engineering and AI language models can help you keep your content fresh, engaging, and relevant to your target audience. By driving greater engagement and results for your marketing campaigns, these tools can help you achieve greater success in your business and achieve your marketing goals.

4.2 Education and Learning

Prompt engineering can be a valuable tool in education and learning, facilitating personalized and adaptive learning experiences for students. In this section, we will discuss various applications of prompt engineering in the context of education and learning.

4.2.1 Adaptive Learning Content

AI language models can be used to create adaptive learning content that adjusts to a student's skill level, learning style, and preferences. By designing prompts that take into account a student's progress and needs, you can generate personalized content that enhances learning outcomes and keeps students engaged.

Example: To create adaptive learning content for a math lesson, you can use a prompt like: "Generate a set of 10 math problems suitable for a [student skill level] student focusing on [specific math topic]. Ensure the problems are varied in difficulty and include detailed solutions for each problem."

4.2.2 Automated Feedback and Grading

AI models can be utilized to provide automated feedback and grading on student assignments, essays, and exams. By crafting prompts that guide the AI model to assess content based on specific criteria and rubrics, you can generate detailed feedback and grading that helps students understand their strengths and areas for improvement.

Example: To provide feedback on an essay, you can use a prompt like: "Evaluate the following essay based on its organization, clarity, evidence, and language use. Provide detailed feedback on each criterion, highlighting strengths and suggesting areas for improvement."

4.2.3 Tutoring and Q&A Support

Prompt engineering can be employed to create AI-powered tutoring systems and Q&A support, offering personalized assistance to students as they work through learning materials or complete assignments. By crafting prompts that guide the AI model to answer questions, explain concepts, or provide step-by-step guidance, you can create a valuable learning resource for students.

Example: To create an AI-powered Q&A support system, you can use a prompt like: "Explain in simple terms how [specific concept] works and provide a real-world example to illustrate its application."

4.2.4 Learning Games and Interactive Content

AI-generated content can be used to create learning games and interactive content that engage and motivate students. By designing prompts that generate game scenarios, puzzles, or challenges, you can create fun and engaging learning experiences that promote knowledge retention and skill development.

Example: To create a learning game for teaching vocabulary, you can use a prompt like: "Generate a crossword puzzle with 15 words related to [specific subject]. Provide clues for each word and ensure the words are appropriate for students at the [target grade level]."

4.2.5 Collaborative Learning and Group Projects

Prompt engineering can facilitate collaborative learning and group projects by generating content that fosters communication, cooperation, and problem-solving among students. By crafting prompts that guide the AI model to create discussion questions, debate topics, or group activities, you can encourage students to work together, share ideas, and learn from one another.

Example: To create a group activity for a history lesson, you can use a prompt like: "Design a group activity for high school students studying the American Revolution. The activity should encourage students to collaborate, research, and discuss different perspectives on the causes, events, and outcomes of the revolution. Provide clear instructions, learning objectives, and a list of resources for students to use during the activity."

By incorporating effective prompt engineering techniques such as scaffolding, questioning, and feedback mechanisms in collaborative learning and group projects, educators can create more engaging, interactive, and dynamic learning experiences. These experiences promote critical thinking, teamwork, and peer-to-peer learning, which can help students develop a wide range of essential skills.

Furthermore, by providing opportunities for students to reflect on their learning and engage in metacognitive processes, educators can deepen their students' understanding of the subject matter. Additionally, this approach fosters a more inclusive and collaborative learning environment, where students can share their diverse perspectives and learn from each other's experiences.

4.3 Customer Support and FAQ Automation

Prompt engineering can be highly useful in customer support and FAQ automation, enabling businesses to provide quick and accurate answers to customer queries. In this section, we will discuss the applications of prompt engineering in the context of customer support and FAQ automation.

4.3.1 Generating Knowledge Base Articles

AI language models can be used to generate knowledge base articles that cover common customer questions, issues, and concerns. By crafting prompts that provide clear guidance on the specific topics and information to be included, you can create comprehensive and easy-to-understand articles that address customer needs.

Example: To create a knowledge base article on troubleshooting a specific product issue, you can use a prompt like: "Write a step-by-step guide to troubleshooting [specific product issue] for [product name]. Include clear instructions, illustrations, and potential solutions to help customers resolve the issue."

4.3.2 Automating FAQ Responses

Prompt engineering can be employed to automate responses to frequently asked questions, providing quick and accurate information to customers. By designing prompts that guide the AI model to answer specific questions based on predefined information, you can generate helpful and relevant responses that improve customer satisfaction.

Example: To automate a response to a common question about product features, you can use a prompt like: "What are the key features of [product name] and how do they benefit users?"

4.3.3 Chatbot and Virtual Assistant Integration

AI-generated content can be integrated into chatbots and virtual assistants to provide personalized and context-aware customer support. By crafting prompts that take into account customer inputs and conversation history, you can generate tailored responses that address customer concerns and enhance the overall support experience.

Example: To create a chatbot response that helps customers track their orders, you can use a prompt like: "Based on the customer's order number [order_number], provide an update on the current status of their order and an estimated delivery date."

4.3.4 Escalation and Handoff to Human Support

In some cases, AI-generated content may not be sufficient to address a customer's issue or concern. Prompt engineering can be used to recognize when a query requires escalation or handoff to a human support representative, ensuring that customers receive the appropriate level of assistance.

Example: To create a chatbot response that escalates a complex issue to human support, you can use a prompt like: "Based on the customer's issue description, if the AI model identifies a complex issue or one that requires personalized assistance, generate a response that informs the customer that their issue will be escalated to a support representative for further assistance."

By incorporating escalation and handoff capabilities into your customer support and FAQ automation efforts, you can ensure that customers receive the right level of support when needed, maintaining high levels of customer satisfaction and trust.

One of the key benefits of incorporating escalation and handoff capabilities is that it allows your support team to focus on high-priority tasks that require human expertise. This will result in a more efficient and effective support experience for your customers. It will also increase customer satisfaction, as they will feel that their concerns are being addressed in a timely manner.

Furthermore, by automating your customer support and FAQ efforts, you can create a more customer-centric support experience. This means that your customers will receive personalized support that is tailored to their specific needs. This personalized support will help to build trust and loyalty with your customers, as they will feel that your company truly cares about their individual needs.

Prompt engineering techniques are also critical in creating an efficient and effective support experience. By using these techniques, you can ensure that your support team is able to respond to customer inquiries and concerns in a timely manner. This will help to reduce wait times and ensure that your customers receive the support they need as quickly as possible.

Overall, incorporating escalation and handoff capabilities, as well as prompt engineering techniques, into your customer support and FAQ automation efforts can have a significant impact on customer satisfaction and trust. By providing personalized support and responding quickly to customer inquiries, you can build strong relationships with your customers and ensure their long-term loyalty to your brand.

4.4 Data Analysis and Visualization

Prompt engineering can play a significant role in data analysis and visualization, enabling users to derive insights from complex data sets and communicate their findings effectively. In this section, we will discuss the applications of prompt engineering in the context of data analysis and visualization.

4.4.1 Summarizing Data Insights

AI language models can be used to generate summaries of key insights and trends within a data set, helping users understand the most important findings and implications. By crafting prompts that guide the AI model to analyze and interpret data, you can create concise and informative summaries that highlight critical information.

Example: To generate a summary of key insights from a sales data set, you can use a prompt like: "Analyze the following sales data set and provide a brief summary of the most important trends, patterns, and insights, including any notable changes in sales performance, customer segments, or product categories."

4.4.2 Suggesting Data Visualizations

Prompt engineering can be employed to suggest appropriate data visualizations that effectively communicate insights and trends within a data set. By designing prompts that guide the AI model to recommend visualization types based on the data structure and user goals, you can generate helpful suggestions that enhance the presentation and understanding of data.

Example: To suggest a suitable data visualization for a given data set, you can use a prompt like: "Given the following data set on website traffic, recommend the most effective data visualization type to display the distribution of traffic sources and explain why this visualization is appropriate for the data."

4.4.3 Natural Language Processing of Data Queries

AI-generated content can be used to process natural language data queries, allowing users to ask questions about their data and receive relevant insights and visualizations in response. By crafting prompts that guide the AI model to understand and respond to user queries, you can create an intuitive and user-friendly data analysis experience.

Example: To create a natural language processing system for data queries, you can use a prompt like: "What was the average revenue per user (ARPU) for [specific product] in the last quarter?"

4.4.4 Generating Data-Driven Narratives

Prompt engineering can be utilized to create data-driven narratives that tell compelling stories based on the insights derived from data analysis. By designing prompts that guide the AI model to weave data insights into a coherent and engaging narrative, you can effectively communicate the significance of your findings to your audience.

Example: To generate a data-driven narrative about the impact of a marketing campaign, you can use a prompt like: "Based on the following data and insights from our recent marketing campaign, create a narrative that highlights the key successes, challenges, and lessons learned. Include specific data points and trends to support your story and make it compelling for the audience."

By incorporating prompt engineering techniques into your data analysis and visualization efforts, you can create data-driven narratives that not only inform but also engage and captivate your audience. By doing so, you can ensure that your stakeholders are able to grasp the value and importance of your data insights, as well as the underlying trends and patterns that you have identified. This can be especially important in more complex or technical fields, as it can help to bridge the gap between technical expertise and broader stakeholder understanding.

For example, imagine that you are working on a data analysis project for a healthcare organization. By incorporating prompt engineering techniques into your analysis and visualization efforts, you can create a narrative that effectively conveys the importance of your insights to the organization's stakeholders, such as patients, doctors, and other healthcare professionals. This can help to foster a deeper understanding of the trends and patterns that you have identified, as well as the value that your insights can bring to the organization as a whole.

In addition, by engaging your audience with data-driven narratives, you can help to create a culture of data-driven decision-making within your organization. This can lead to more informed and effective decision-making across a variety of fields, from healthcare to finance to marketing and beyond. Ultimately, by incorporating prompt engineering techniques into your data analysis and visualization efforts, you can help to drive positive change and improve outcomes for your organization and its stakeholders.

4.5 Content Creation and Marketing

Prompt engineering can significantly contribute to content creation and marketing efforts, enabling businesses and individuals to generate engaging, relevant, and high-quality content at scale. In this section, we will discuss the applications of prompt engineering in the context of content creation and marketing.

4.5.1 Blog Post and Article Generation

AI language models can be used to generate blog posts and articles on various topics, providing valuable content for your audience. By crafting prompts that outline the desired subject matter, structure, and tone, you can create informative and engaging content that resonates with your readers.

Example: To generate a blog post about the latest trends in digital marketing, you can use a prompt like: "Write a 1,000-word blog post discussing the top 5 digital marketing trends to watch in 2023. Provide an overview of each trend, its significance, and practical tips for businesses to leverage these trends effectively."

4.5.2 Social Media Content Creation

Prompt engineering can be employed to create captivating social media content that drives engagement and brand awareness. By designing prompts that guide the AI model to generate platform-specific content, such as Tweets, Facebook posts, or Instagram captions, you can create a consistent and compelling social media presence.

Example: To create a Tweet promoting a new product launch, you can use a prompt like: "Craft an engaging and attention-grabbing Tweet announcing the launch of [product name] and highlighting its key features and benefits. Use a tone that is consistent with our brand voice."

4.5.3 Email Marketing Campaigns

AI-generated content can be integrated into email marketing campaigns to create personalized and targeted messages that resonate with your subscribers. By crafting prompts that take into account user preferences, purchase history, and other relevant data, you can generate tailored content that drives engagement and conversions.

Example: To create a personalized email promoting a special offer, you can use a prompt like: "Based on the customer's previous purchases and browsing history, write a personalized email promoting a limited-time offer on related products. Include a clear call-to-action and a sense of urgency to encourage the customer to take advantage of the offer."

4.5.4 SEO-Optimized Content

Prompt engineering can be used to generate SEO-optimized content that helps improve search engine rankings and drive organic traffic to your website. By crafting prompts that guide the AI model to include targeted keywords, relevant internal and external links, and a clear and concise structure, you can create content that is both engaging for your audience and optimized for search engines.

Example: To generate an SEO-optimized article about sustainable fashion, you can use a prompt like: "Write a 1,200-word SEO-optimized article on the topic of sustainable fashion. Include the following keywords: 'sustainable fashion,' 'ethical clothing,' and 'eco-friendly materials.' Discuss the importance of sustainable fashion, highlight popular sustainable brands, and provide tips for consumers to make more environmentally conscious choices."

By incorporating prompt engineering techniques into your content creation and marketing efforts, you can generate SEO-optimized content that helps improve your search engine rankings, drive organic traffic, and ultimately, reach a wider audience. One way to achieve this is by conducting thorough keyword research, identifying high-volume keywords relevant to your target audience, and incorporating them strategically into your content. Additionally, you can create long-form content that provides in-depth information on your industry or topics of interest to your audience.

This type of content is more likely to be shared and linked to by others, further boosting your search engine rankings and increasing your visibility. By regularly producing high-quality, informative content, you can establish your brand as a thought leader in your industry and build trust with your audience. This, in turn, can lead to increased user engagement, higher conversion rates, and ultimately, greater business success.

By mastering prompt engineering techniques, you can harness the power of AI language models to enhance your content creation and marketing efforts. This can help you generate high-quality, engaging, and relevant content at scale, ultimately improving your brand's visibility, driving customer engagement, and increasing conversions.

4.6 Personalized Learning and Educational Content

Prompt engineering can play a significant role in personalized learning and educational content, allowing educators and learners to create tailored materials and resources that cater to individual needs, preferences, and learning styles. In this section, we will discuss the applications of prompt engineering in the context of personalized learning and educational content.

4.6.1 Customized Study Materials

AI language models can be used to generate customized study materials that focus on specific topics, concepts, or learning objectives, helping students master the content more effectively. By crafting prompts that outline the desired subject matter, structure, and difficulty level, you can create study materials that meet the unique needs of individual learners.

Example: To generate a customized study guide for a high school physics student, you can use a prompt like: "Create a study guide for a high school student focusing on the topic of electromagnetism. Cover key concepts such as magnetic fields, electromagnetic induction, and Faraday's law. Include clear explanations, diagrams, and sample problems with step-by-step solutions."

4.6.2 Adaptive Learning Assessments

Prompt engineering can be employed to create adaptive learning assessments that adjust the difficulty and focus of questions based on a student's performance. By designing prompts that guide the AI model to generate questions that match the learner's skill level and progress, you can create assessments that provide accurate and actionable feedback to support continued learning and growth.

Example: To create an adaptive learning assessment for a mathematics student, you can use a prompt like: "Generate a series of math problems covering topics in algebra, geometry, and trigonometry. Adjust the difficulty and focus of the questions based on the student's performance, providing more challenging problems when they demonstrate mastery and offering additional support when they struggle with a concept."

4.6.3 Personalized Learning Plans

AI-generated content can be used to develop personalized learning plans that outline a tailored learning path for individual students, taking into account their strengths, weaknesses, and goals. By crafting prompts that consider the learner's academic history, preferences, and objectives, you can generate learning plans that optimize their educational experience and support their success.

Example: To create a personalized learning plan for a student aiming to improve their writing skills, you can use a prompt like: "Based on the student's writing samples, areas of strength, and areas needing improvement, create a personalized learning plan that outlines a series of writing exercises, resources, and goals to help them enhance their writing skills over the next three months."

4.6.4 Tutoring and Homework Assistance

Prompt engineering can be utilized to provide tutoring and homework assistance to students, offering guidance and support on specific questions or challenges they may encounter during their studies. By designing prompts that guide the AI model to understand the student's question, provide step-by-step explanations, and offer tips for future success, you can create a valuable tutoring resource that supplements the learner's educational experience.

Example: To provide homework assistance on a calculus problem, you can use a prompt like: "The student is struggling with the following calculus problem: 'Find the derivative of $f(x) = 3x^2 + 5x - 2$.' Provide a step-by-step explanation of how to solve the problem and offer tips on how to approach similar problems in the future."

By mastering prompt engineering techniques, you can harness the power of AI language models to enhance personalized learning and educational content, creating tailored materials and resources that cater to individual learners' needs and preferences.

For instance, you can use prompt engineering to tailor the difficulty level of the learning materials to match the skill level of the students. You can also use it to identify the specific areas where students struggle the most and provide additional resources for those areas. Additionally, prompt engineering can help you create more engaging and interactive learning experiences, such as gamification and simulations.

By embracing prompt engineering techniques, educators can create a more personalized and effective learning environment that can help students achieve a deeper understanding of the subject matter, foster greater engagement with learning, and ultimately, support their long-term academic success.

4.7 Customer Support and Chatbots

Prompt engineering can be effectively used in customer support and chatbots, allowing businesses to create AI-driven solutions that offer responsive, personalized, and efficient assistance to customers. In this section, we will discuss the applications of prompt engineering in the context of customer support and chatbots.

4.7.1 Handling Frequently Asked Questions (FAQs)

AI language models can be used to handle FAQs by providing accurate and helpful responses to common customer inquiries. By crafting prompts that guide the AI model to understand the customer's question and provide a relevant, concise, and informative answer, you can create a valuable resource for addressing customer concerns.

Example: To create a chatbot response for a question about shipping times, you can use a prompt like: "The customer is asking about the estimated shipping time for their order. Provide a response that explains our standard shipping times, factors that may affect delivery, and how the customer can track their order."

4.7.2 Personalized Product Recommendations

Prompt engineering can be employed to generate personalized product recommendations for customers based on their preferences, purchase history, and other relevant data. By designing prompts that guide the AI model to analyze customer information and suggest suitable products, you can create a tailored shopping experience that boosts customer satisfaction and drives sales.

Example: To create a chatbot that offers personalized product recommendations, you can use a prompt like: "Based on the customer's browsing history and previous purchases, recommend three products that they may be interested in. Provide a brief description of each product and explain why it may be a good fit for the customer."

4.7.3 Troubleshooting and Technical Support

AI-generated content can be used to provide troubleshooting and technical support for customers experiencing issues with a product or service. By crafting prompts that guide the AI model to understand the problem, offer step-by-step solutions, and follow up with additional assistance if needed, you can create an effective support resource that addresses customer issues efficiently.

Example: To create a chatbot response for a customer experiencing issues with a software application, you can use a prompt like: "The customer is having trouble installing our software on their computer. Provide a step-by-step guide to troubleshooting the installation process and offer additional support options if the issue persists."

4.7.4 Proactive Support and Customer Engagement

Prompt engineering can be utilized to create AI-driven proactive support and customer engagement strategies that anticipate customer needs and offer timely assistance. By designing prompts that guide the AI model to analyze customer data, identify potential concerns, and provide relevant information or support, you can create a more engaging and satisfying customer experience.

Example: To create a chatbot that offers proactive support for a customer approaching their data usage limit, you can use a prompt like: "The customer is nearing their monthly data usage limit. Notify the customer of their current data usage, provide tips on how to reduce data consumption, and offer options for upgrading their plan to avoid overage charges."

By mastering prompt engineering techniques, you can harness the power of AI language models to enhance customer support and chatbot experiences. This can help you create responsive, personalized, and efficient solutions that address customer concerns, boost satisfaction, and ultimately, drive loyalty and growth for your business.

With the increasing demand for customer support services, businesses need to adopt more advanced methods to provide prompt and effective solutions. AI language models have emerged as a viable solution to automate customer support services and provide personalized responses to customers. Prompt engineering techniques help businesses leverage the power of AI language models to create responsive and efficient chatbots that can handle a wide range of customer queries, from simple to complex.

By mastering prompt engineering techniques, businesses can develop chatbots that can provide personalized responses, anticipate customer needs, and resolve issues quickly. This can lead to greater customer satisfaction, increased loyalty, and ultimately, business growth. Additionally, businesses can gain valuable insights into customer behavior and preferences by analyzing chatbot interactions, which can inform product development and marketing strategies.

In short, prompt engineering techniques can help businesses unlock the full potential of AI language models to provide exceptional customer support and drive business growth.

4.8 Journalism and Content Creation

Prompt engineering can be applied effectively in journalism and content creation, allowing writers and editors to leverage AI language models to generate engaging, informative, and accurate articles or stories. In this section, we will discuss the applications of prompt engineering in the context of journalism and content creation.

4.8.1 Generating News Summaries

AI language models can be used to generate concise news summaries that provide readers with a quick and accurate overview of current events or stories. By crafting prompts that guide the AI model to extract the most important information from an article or news source, you can create news summaries that are both informative and engaging.

Example: To generate a news summary from a recent article, you can use a prompt like: "Summarize the key points of the following article in a 150-word summary, highlighting the main events, people involved, and the potential implications of the story."

4.8.2 Writing Op-Eds and Analytical Pieces

Prompt engineering can be employed to create op-eds and analytical pieces that explore different perspectives, opinions, and ideas related to a specific topic or issue. By designing prompts that guide the AI model to consider various viewpoints, arguments, and evidence, you can generate thought-provoking content that sparks conversation and debate.

Example: To create an op-ed discussing the impact of artificial intelligence on the job market, you can use a prompt like: "Write an op-ed discussing the potential effects of artificial intelligence on the job market. Explore both the positive and negative implications, and consider the perspectives of employers, employees, and policymakers."

4.8.3 Creative Storytelling and Fiction

AI-generated content can be used to develop creative stories and fiction pieces that entertain and inspire readers. By crafting prompts that outline the desired setting, characters, plot, and theme, you can create compelling narratives that capture the imagination of your audience.

Example: To generate a science fiction short story, you can use a prompt like: "Write a 2,000-word science fiction short story set on a distant planet inhabited by intelligent alien life forms. The story should explore themes of cultural exchange, communication, and the challenges of interstellar diplomacy."

4.8.4 Fact-Checking and Source Verification

Prompt engineering can be employed to assist journalists in fact-checking and verifying the accuracy of information and sources. By designing prompts that guide the AI model to evaluate the reliability of a piece of information or the credibility of a source, you can create a valuable tool that helps journalists maintain high standards of accuracy and integrity in their reporting.

Example: To create a prompt that assists with fact-checking a statement made by a politician, you can use a prompt like: "Fact-check the following statement made by [Politician Name]: '[Quote from the politician].' Investigate the accuracy of the statement by referring to reputable sources and provide a brief analysis of the findings."

By mastering prompt engineering techniques, you can harness the power of AI language models to enhance journalism and content creation. With the use of AI, you can generate engaging, informative, and accurate articles, stories, and other written content. The use of AI can lead to increased readership, a wider audience, and greater impact for your work. This not only benefits the writer but the readers as well.

AI-generated content can provide readers with more relevant and personalized content, which can lead to a better user experience. Additionally, AI can help writers save time by automating certain tasks, allowing them to focus on more creative work. It's clear that AI is changing the way we create and consume content, and by mastering prompt engineering techniques, you can stay ahead of the curve and take advantage of these powerful tools.

4.9 Social Media and Online Marketing

Prompt engineering can be effectively applied in the realm of social media and online marketing, allowing businesses and marketers to leverage AI language models to create engaging, targeted, and persuasive content. In this section, we will discuss the applications of prompt engineering in the context of social media and online marketing.

4.9.1 Generating Social Media Content

AI language models can be used to generate social media content that resonates with audiences and encourages interaction. By crafting prompts that guide the AI model to understand the target audience, their preferences, and the desired tone or message, you can create social media posts that drive engagement and brand awareness.

Example: To generate a social media post promoting a new product, you can use a prompt like: "Create a 280-character tweet promoting the launch of our new eco-friendly backpack, highlighting its sustainable materials, unique design features, and special launch discount."

4.9.2 Crafting Compelling Ad Copy

Prompt engineering can be employed to create persuasive ad copy that effectively communicates the value proposition of a product or service and motivates potential customers to take action. By designing prompts that guide the AI model to consider the target audience, the benefits of the product or service, and the desired call-to-action, you can generate impactful advertising content that drives conversions.

Example: To create ad copy for a pay-per-click (PPC) campaign, you can use a prompt like: "Write a 90-character Google Ads headline and a 150-character description for our online fitness coaching service, emphasizing the personalized training plans, expert coaching, and flexible scheduling options."

4.9.3 Influencer Marketing and Collaboration

AI-generated content can be used to identify and reach out to potential influencers or collaborators in your industry or niche. By crafting prompts that guide the AI model to analyze social media profiles, evaluate the relevance and reach of potential partners, and craft personalized outreach messages, you can create effective influencer marketing campaigns that expand your brand's reach and influence.

Example: To generate a list of potential influencers and personalized outreach messages, you can use a prompt like: "Identify five influencers in the health and wellness space who have a strong engagement rate and a follower count between 10,000 and 50,000. For each influencer, provide a brief description of their content focus and draft a personalized message proposing a collaboration with our brand."

4.9.4 Content Curation and Recommendation

Prompt engineering can be used to create AI-driven content curation and recommendation tools that help businesses and marketers discover, analyze, and share relevant content with their target audiences. By designing prompts that guide the AI model to evaluate the quality, relevance, and potential interest of content within a specific industry or niche, you can create a valuable resource that keeps your audience engaged and informed.

Example: To create a content curation tool that discovers and evaluates articles related to digital marketing trends, you can use a prompt like: "Find three high-quality articles published within the last week discussing the latest trends in digital marketing. Provide a brief summary of each article, highlighting the key insights and takeaways, and explain why they are relevant to our audience."

Incorporating prompt engineering techniques into social media and online marketing is a powerful way to leverage the capabilities of AI-powered content curation and recommendation tools. These tools can help businesses and marketers more effectively discover, analyze, and share relevant content with their target audiences.

By regularly curating and recommending high-quality content, these tools can drive increased user engagement, improve brand awareness, and foster greater customer loyalty. In the long run, these benefits can provide a significant boost to your business's overall success and profitability.

4.10 Education and eLearning

Prompt engineering can be effectively applied in the field of education and eLearning, allowing educators, students, and content creators to leverage AI language models to create engaging, informative, and personalized learning experiences. In this section, we will discuss the applications of prompt engineering in the context of education and eLearning.

4.10.1 Generating Study Materials

AI language models can be used to generate study materials, such as summaries, flashcards, or quizzes, that help students understand and retain information more effectively. By crafting prompts that guide the AI model to extract key concepts, terms, or ideas from a given topic, you can create customized study materials that cater to the specific needs and learning styles of your students.

Example: To create a set of flashcards on a biology topic, you can use a prompt like: "Generate 10 flashcards for the topic of cellular respiration, including a question and answer for each card. Ensure the questions cover essential concepts, processes, and terminology related to cellular respiration."

4.10.2 Providing Personalized Feedback

Prompt engineering can be employed to create AI-powered feedback tools that provide personalized guidance and support to students as they complete assignments or assessments. By designing prompts that guide the AI model to evaluate a student's work, identify areas for improvement, and offer constructive feedback, you can create an effective learning tool that helps students grow and develop their skills.

Example: To provide personalized feedback on a student's essay, you can use a prompt like: "Review the following student essay and provide feedback on the strengths and weaknesses of the content, organization, and writing style. Offer specific suggestions for improvement and encourage the student to address these areas in their revision."

4.10.3 Developing Interactive Learning Activities

AI-generated content can be used to create interactive learning activities, such as simulations, games, or scenarios, that engage students and promote deeper understanding of complex concepts. By crafting prompts that outline the desired learning objectives, context, and mechanics, you can create immersive educational experiences that cater to various learning styles and preferences.

Example: To create an interactive learning activity for teaching programming concepts, you can use a prompt like: "Design a text-based adventure game that teaches basic programming concepts, such as variables, loops, and conditional statements. Describe the game's storyline, setting, and key challenges, and explain how players will apply programming concepts to solve problems and progress through the game."

4.10.4 AI-Assisted Language Learning

Prompt engineering can be used to create AI-powered language learning tools that help students practice and improve their language skills in a more interactive and engaging way. By designing prompts that guide the AI model to generate language exercises, offer corrections, and provide explanations, you can create a personalized language tutor that adapts to the needs and proficiency level of each student.

Example: To create a language learning exercise for practicing verb conjugation in French, you can use a prompt like: "Generate a set of 10 fill-in-the-blank sentences to practice the conjugation of the verb 'avoir' in the present tense. Include the correct conjugation in parentheses after each blank, and provide a brief explanation for each conjugation rule."

Mastering prompt engineering techniques is essential for leveraging the full potential of AI language models in the field of education and eLearning. These techniques enable educators to create highly engaging, informative, and personalized learning materials that can cater to the diverse needs and preferences of students. By providing a more personalized and interactive learning experience, students are more likely to remain engaged and motivated to learn. This can lead to improved learning outcomes, including higher retention rates and increased mastery of key concepts.

Moreover, the use of prompt engineering techniques can also help educators to identify and address knowledge gaps more effectively.

By analyzing the responses of students to different prompts, educators can gain valuable insights into their students' learning progress and adapt their teaching strategies accordingly. This can help to ensure that students are receiving the support and guidance they need to succeed in their educational endeavors.

In addition to improving learning outcomes, the use of prompt engineering techniques can also lead to increased student satisfaction. By providing a more personalized and interactive learning experience, students are more likely to feel valued and supported in their learning journey. This can help to foster a positive learning environment and encourage students to take an active role in their own learning.

Overall, mastering prompt engineering techniques is a powerful tool for educators and eLearning professionals looking to enhance the quality and effectiveness of their teaching. By leveraging the power of AI language models, educators can create highly engaging, informative, and personalized learning materials that can cater to the diverse needs and preferences of students, leading to improved learning outcomes, increased student satisfaction, and greater success in educational endeavors.

CHAPTER 5: Iterative Prompt Design Process

In the world of prompt engineering, the key to achieving optimal results lies in the iterative prompt design process. This process involves designing an initial prompt, evaluating its performance, identifying areas for improvement, and making adjustments accordingly.

To design an effective prompt, you need to consider various factors such as the target audience, the context of application, the desired outcomes, and the available resources. You need to analyze the language model's strengths and weaknesses and identify the domain-specific knowledge that it lacks. You need to evaluate the prompt's effectiveness based on multiple criteria such as accuracy, relevance, completeness, and coherence.

Once you have designed the initial prompt, you need to test it against a diverse set of inputs and outputs. You need to measure its performance based on various metrics such as precision, recall, F1 score, and perplexity. You need to identify the patterns of errors and the sources of confusion and ambiguity. You need to gather feedback from the users and the domain experts and incorporate their suggestions into the prompt design.

Based on the evaluation results, you need to identify the areas for improvement and make appropriate adjustments to the prompt. You need to modify the language patterns, the domain knowledge, the input and output formats, and the training data. You need to experiment with different variations of the prompt and compare their performance. You need to track the progress of the prompt over time and monitor its stability and consistency.

By continuously refining the prompt, you can ensure that the AI language model generates the desired outputs that are both accurate and effective. In this chapter, we will delve into the iterative prompt design process and explore techniques for evaluating and refining prompts, with a focus on practical examples and real-world applications.

5.1 Setting Clear Goals for the Prompt

The iterative prompt design process begins with setting clear goals for the prompt. This involves defining the purpose of the prompt, the type of output you expect from the AI model, and any specific requirements or constraints that need to be considered. By establishing clear goals upfront, you can create a solid foundation for designing effective prompts and refining them through the iterative process.

When setting goals for your prompt, consider the following aspects:

1. Purpose: What do you want to achieve with the AI-generated output? This could be to answer a question, provide information, offer suggestions, or create engaging content.
2. Output format: Define the format you expect from the AI-generated output. This could include the structure, style, or tone of the content. For example, you may want a list of bullet points, a brief summary, or a more detailed explanation.
3. Specific requirements: Identify any specific requirements or constraints that the AI-generated output must adhere to. This could include word limits, the inclusion of certain keywords or phrases, or the need to avoid sensitive or inappropriate content.

Example: Imagine you want to create a prompt that generates a list of tips for improving time management skills. Before designing the prompt, set clear goals, such as:

1. Purpose: Provide useful and actionable tips for improving time management skills.
2. Output format: A list of 5-7 concise bullet points.
3. Specific requirements: Each tip should be phrased as an actionable step and avoid using jargon or overly technical language.
4. Prioritization: In cases where multiple goals or objectives are involved, prioritize them according to their importance. This can help you focus on the most crucial aspects of your prompt and ensure that the AI-generated output addresses the most important points.
5. Flexibility: While setting clear goals is essential, it's also important to remain open to adjusting these goals as you iterate and refine your prompt. As you learn more about the AI model's capabilities and limitations, you may need to revisit your goals and adjust them accordingly to achieve the best possible results.
6. Collaboration: If you're working with a team, make sure to communicate your goals and objectives clearly to all team members. This helps ensure that everyone is on the same page and can contribute effectively to the prompt design process.

By taking into account the following aspects, you can expand the prompt design process to be more comprehensive and adaptable, thereby increasing the likelihood of successfully generating the desired AI-generated outputs.

Firstly, it is important to analyze the type of data that will be used to train the AI model. Different types of data require different treatment and processing methods, and this can greatly impact the outcome of the AI-generated outputs.

Secondly, it is essential to consider the context in which the AI-generated outputs will be utilized. This can include factors such as target audience, specific use cases, and industry-specific terminology.

Thirdly, it can be beneficial to conduct user testing and gather feedback to continuously improve the prompt design process. This can help to identify areas of improvement and refine the process for generating more effective AI-generated outputs.

By incorporating these additional considerations into the prompt design process, you can create a more robust and effective system for generating the desired AI-generated outputs.

5.2 Drafting an Initial Prompt

Once you have set clear goals for your prompt, the next step in the iterative prompt design process is to draft an initial prompt. This involves crafting a prompt that communicates your goals to the AI model and encourages it to generate the desired output.

When drafting an initial prompt, consider the following guidelines:

Be specific:

Provide clear instructions and specify the format, structure, or style you expect from the AI-generated output. This helps the AI model understand your requirements and tailor its response accordingly.

Example: Instead of asking, "Tell me about time management tips," you could ask, "Provide a list of 5-7 concise and actionable tips for improving time management skills."

Provide context:

Giving the AI model some context can help it generate more relevant and accurate outputs. Include relevant background information or set the scene to guide the AI model's understanding of the prompt.

Example: "As a busy professional trying to balance work and personal life, provide a list of 5-7 concise and actionable tips for improving time management skills."

Use leading questions or phrases:

If you want the AI model to explore specific aspects or ideas, consider using leading questions or phrases to guide its response.

Example: "Considering the challenges faced by remote workers, provide a list of 5-7 concise and actionable tips for improving time management skills while working from home."

Test with different prompt styles:

If you're unsure which prompt style will yield the best results, experiment with different styles, such as open-ended questions, fill-in-the-blank statements, or declarative instructions.

Examples:

- "What are some effective time management tips for remote workers?"
- "Complete the following sentence: One useful time management tip for remote workers is _____."

Keep it concise:

While providing context and specific instructions is important, try to keep your prompt concise and to the point. Overly long or complex prompts can sometimes confuse the AI model or dilute the focus of the generated output.

Avoid ambiguous language:

Use clear and unambiguous language to minimize the chances of misinterpretation by the AI model. Ambiguities in the prompt can lead to unexpected or off-topic responses.

Adjust the level of detail:

Depending on your goals and the AI model's capabilities, you may need to provide more or less detail in your prompt. Experiment with the level of detail to find the right balance that yields the desired output.

Include examples (if necessary):

If you have specific expectations for the output, consider providing an example within the prompt. This can help guide the AI model and give it a clearer idea of what you're looking for.

Example: "Provide a list of 5-7 concise and actionable tips for improving time management skills while working from home. For example, one tip could be setting specific working hours to create a clear boundary between work and personal time."

By taking the time to carefully consider these additional tips and implementing them into your initial prompt, you can significantly enhance the quality and accuracy of the AI-generated outputs that you receive during the iterative prompt design process. By refining your prompt in this way, you will be able to better articulate your goals and objectives, and provide the AI with a clearer understanding of what you hope to achieve with its assistance.

This will allow the AI to more effectively analyze and synthesize the available data, and generate outputs that are better aligned with your desired outcomes. So whether you're developing a new product or service, conducting research, or exploring new business opportunities, incorporating these tips into your prompt development process can help you achieve better results and unlock new possibilities for growth and success.

5.3 Evaluating and Analyzing AI-generated Outputs

After drafting an initial prompt, the next step in the iterative prompt design process is to evaluate and analyze the AI-generated outputs. This involves examining the generated content to determine if it meets your goals, requirements, and expectations, and identifying areas for improvement.

When evaluating and analyzing AI-generated outputs, consider the following guidelines:

Relevance:

Assess whether the generated content is relevant to your prompt and addresses the main points or questions you posed. If the AI model is generating irrelevant or off-topic content, you may need to revise your prompt to provide clearer instructions or context.

Accuracy:

Check the generated content for factual accuracy and consistency with any background information provided in the prompt. If you find inaccuracies, consider refining your prompt or providing additional context to guide the AI model.

Structure and format:

Evaluate the structure and format of the AI-generated output to ensure it aligns with your goals and requirements. If the output deviates from the desired format, you may need to provide more specific instructions or examples in your prompt.

Style and tone:

Review the style and tone of the generated content to ensure it matches your desired tone, such as formal, conversational, or persuasive. If the tone is off, consider adjusting your prompt to provide guidance on the desired tone.

Completeness:

Determine if the AI-generated output sufficiently covers the topic or addresses all aspects of your prompt. If some aspects are missing or underdeveloped, you may need to revise your prompt to emphasize those areas.

Identify patterns and biases:

Be mindful of any patterns, biases, or limitations in the AI-generated outputs. If you notice the model consistently generating content with certain biases or inaccuracies, consider addressing these issues in your prompt or during the post-processing stage.

Example: After evaluating an AI-generated list of time management tips, you notice that the tips are relevant and accurate but not as actionable as you had hoped. In this case, you might revise your prompt to emphasize the need for actionable steps and provide a clearer example of what you're looking for.

Creativity and novelty:

Consider whether the generated content offers creative or novel insights, especially when seeking innovative solutions or fresh perspectives. If the output seems generic or repetitive, try adjusting your prompt to encourage more original thinking.

Readability and coherence:

Assess the readability and coherence of the generated content. The output should be easy to understand and follow a logical flow of ideas. If the content is difficult to read or lacks coherence, consider refining your prompt to address these issues.

Iterative feedback:

If you're working with a team, share the AI-generated outputs and your evaluations with your colleagues. Collecting feedback from multiple perspectives can help you identify areas for improvement more effectively.

Balance prompt iterations:

While iterating on your prompt is essential for improvement, be mindful not to over-engineer it. Continuously refining a prompt may lead to diminishing returns, and in some cases, it may be more efficient to accept minor imperfections in the output and address them during the post-processing stage.

When it comes to evaluating and analyzing AI-generated outputs, it's important to take into account a variety of factors. For example, you might think about the context in which the content was generated, including the data that was used to train the AI model. Additionally, you might consider the intended audience for the content, as this can impact how the content is received and interpreted.

Furthermore, it's important to remember that AI-generated content is not infallible, and it may produce outputs that are inaccurate or inappropriate. Therefore, it's important to approach AI-generated content with a critical eye, and be prepared to revise and refine your prompts as needed to achieve the best possible results.

By considering these additional aspects while evaluating and analyzing AI-generated outputs, you can gain a more comprehensive understanding of the content and further refine your prompt to achieve better results in the iterative prompt design process. Ultimately, this can help you to create more accurate, effective, and impactful content, whether you're working on a marketing campaign, developing educational materials, or conducting research in a particular field.

5.4 Refining and Retesting Prompts

After evaluating and analyzing the AI-generated outputs, it is important to take the necessary time to fully examine the results and determine what changes, if any, need to be made to the prompts. This is a crucial part of the iterative prompt design process, as refining and retesting your prompts can lead to a more effective and successful outcome.

When refining your prompts, it is important to keep in mind the specific parameters that are most important to you and your goals. This may involve making adjustments to the wording or structure of the prompt, or even incorporating new information or data into the prompt. Once you have made these adjustments, it is important to retest the modified prompt with the AI model to generate new outputs.

By taking the time to thoroughly evaluate and refine your prompts, you can ensure that you are getting the best possible results from your AI model. This can lead to a better understanding of your data, as well as more accurate and reliable outputs that can be used to inform your decision-making process.

When refining and retesting prompts, consider the following guidelines:

Address identified issues:

Revise your prompt to address the issues you identified during the evaluation and analysis stage. This might involve clarifying instructions, providing additional context, adjusting the tone, or emphasizing specific aspects.

Example: If the AI-generated tips were not actionable enough, revise the prompt by explicitly requesting actionable tips and providing a clearer example: "Provide a list of 5-7 actionable tips for improving time management skills while working from home, with each tip outlining a specific action that can be taken. For example, 'Schedule regular breaks throughout the day to recharge and maintain focus.'"

Test multiple prompt variations:

If you're unsure which prompt revisions will yield the best results, create multiple variations of your prompt and test each one with the AI model. This can help you identify the most effective prompt for achieving your goals.

Re-evaluate and analyze:

After generating new outputs with your refined prompt, repeat the evaluation and analysis process to assess the quality of the new content. This will help you determine if your prompt revisions were effective and whether further refinement is needed.

Iterate as needed:

The iterative prompt design process may require several rounds of refinement and retesting. Continue iterating on your prompt until you achieve the desired output quality. However, be mindful of the balance between refining prompts and addressing minor issues during post-processing.

Document your findings:

As you iterate through the prompt design process, document your findings, including successful prompt variations and the issues they addressed. This can help you develop a deeper understanding of effective prompt design and provide valuable insights for future projects.

Be patient and persistent:

Refining prompts and achieving the desired results can take time and multiple iterations. Be patient and persistent throughout the process, as improving the quality of AI-generated outputs often requires trial and error.

Learn from failures:

If a prompt revision doesn't yield the desired results, treat it as a learning opportunity. Analyze why the revision didn't work and use this information to inform your next iteration.

Experiment with different approaches:

Don't be afraid to experiment with different approaches to prompt design. Trying unconventional techniques or perspectives can sometimes lead to surprising improvements in the AI-generated outputs.

Leverage AI model settings:

In addition to refining your prompt, consider adjusting the AI model's settings, such as temperature and max tokens, to influence the generated output. For example, a lower temperature may yield more focused and conservative results, while a higher temperature may lead to more creative and diverse outputs.

Collaborate with others:

If you're working with a team, collaborate with your colleagues throughout the refinement and retesting process. Sharing ideas and insights can lead to more effective prompt revisions and a deeper understanding of prompt engineering.

By refining and retesting your prompts in an iterative manner, you can continuously improve the AI-generated outputs, ultimately achieving your desired results and mastering the art of prompt engineering.

One of the key benefits of iterative refinement is that it allows you to test and experiment with different prompt variations. This can help you identify which prompts are most effective in generating the desired outputs, and which may need further tweaking or refining.

Furthermore, as you continue to refine your prompts, you may discover new insights and patterns in the AI-generated outputs. These insights can be used to further optimize your prompts, and to gain a deeper understanding of how the AI system operates.

In addition to iterative refinement, another useful technique for improving AI-generated outputs is to leverage external data sources. By incorporating additional data into the AI system, you can expand its knowledge base and improve its ability to generate high-quality outputs.

Overall, mastering the art of prompt engineering requires a combination of iterative refinement, experimentation, and data-driven optimization. By following these best practices, you can achieve your desired results and unlock the full potential of AI-powered content creation.

5.5 Post-processing AI-generated Outputs

After refining your prompt and generating high-quality AI outputs, it is important to remember that post-processing is a crucial step in ensuring that the final content meets your requirements. This step involves carefully examining the AI-generated content and making any necessary edits, reorganizing or adjustments to achieve the desired outcome.

Some examples of post-processing include tweaking the language to improve clarity, adjusting the tone to better suit your target audience, and rearranging the content to create a more logical flow. Additionally, you may want to add in some extra information or examples to further expand on key ideas and ensure that the content is comprehensive and engaging.

Consider the following guidelines for post-processing AI-generated outputs:

Proofread and edit:

Carefully proofread the AI-generated content for grammatical errors, typos, or inconsistencies, and edit as necessary. AI models can sometimes make mistakes or generate awkward phrasings that require correction.

Fact-check:

Verify the factual accuracy of the generated content, especially when it comes to statistics, dates, or other specific details. AI models can generate incorrect or outdated information, so it's essential to double-check these aspects.

Ensure coherence and flow:

Review the coherence and flow of the AI-generated output. You may need to reorganize or restructure the content to improve readability and ensure a logical progression of ideas.

Remove or replace problematic content:

If the AI-generated output contains any problematic, inappropriate, or biased content, remove or replace it to align with your goals and guidelines.

Optimize for your audience:

Tailor the AI-generated content to your specific audience by adapting the language, style, or tone as needed. This may involve simplifying technical jargon, adjusting the level of formality, or incorporating specific terminology used by your target audience.

Incorporate additional insights or context:

If the AI-generated output lacks certain insights or context you deem important, you can add these elements during the post-processing stage to enhance the overall quality and value of the content.

Example: Suppose you used the AI to generate a blog post on time management tips. After refining the prompt and generating the output, you might need to edit the text for grammar, fact-check the information, restructure some sections for better flow, and add an introduction and conclusion to create a cohesive piece.

By carefully post-processing AI-generated outputs, you can ensure the content meets your final requirements and aligns with your goals, even if the AI model did not generate a perfect result initially. This step is crucial in producing high-quality content and mastering the art of prompt engineering.

Therefore, it is important to have a systematic approach to post-processing. One approach is to first read through the AI-generated output and identify any errors or areas that need improvement.

Then, make edits to the content to enhance its clarity and coherence. Additionally, you can add relevant information to the content to make it more informative and engaging for the reader. By following these steps, you can transform an imperfect AI-generated output into a polished and high-quality piece of content that meets your needs and goals.

CHAPTER 6: Advanced Prompt Engineering Strategies

As you become more experienced with prompt engineering, you can start to explore advanced strategies to further improve the AI-generated outputs and tackle more complex tasks. In this chapter, we'll delve into some of these advanced techniques and best practices that can help you achieve even better results. By learning how to optimize the input prompt, you can improve the quality and relevance of the generated text. Additionally, you can learn how to fine-tune the AI model by providing relevant training data, which can help the system understand the nuances of the language and generate more accurate outputs.

Moreover, we'll explore some of the best practices when it comes to using AI-generated text, such as proofreading and fact-checking, to ensure that the outputs are accurate and relevant. Finally, we'll discuss some of the ethical considerations when using AI-generated text, such as bias and fairness, and how to address these issues. By mastering these advanced techniques, you'll be able to take your AI-generated text to the next level and tackle even more complex tasks with ease.

6.1 Systematic Prompt Exploration

Systematic prompt exploration involves a more structured and organized approach to testing and refining prompts to optimize the AI-generated outputs. This method can help you uncover new insights and identify the most effective prompts for your specific use case.

To perform systematic prompt exploration, follow these steps:

Develop a hypothesis:

Start by developing a hypothesis about what kind of prompt might produce the desired output. This hypothesis should be based on your understanding of the AI model and the problem you are trying to solve.

Example: You might hypothesize that providing more explicit instructions in the prompt will lead to better AI-generated summaries of scientific articles.

Design multiple prompt variations:

Based on your hypothesis, design multiple variations of your prompt that systematically explore different aspects of your hypothesis. Each variation should test a specific aspect of your hypothesis.

Example: You can create prompt variations with different levels of explicitness, such as:

- Variation 1: "Summarize the following scientific article."
- Variation 2: "Summarize the following scientific article, focusing on the main findings and implications."
- Variation 3: "Summarize the following scientific article in 3-5 sentences, highlighting the study's goals, methods, results, and conclusions."

Test the prompt variations:.

Use the AI model to generate outputs for each prompt variation. Be sure to collect enough samples for each variation to make a meaningful comparison.

Evaluate and compare the results:

Assess the quality of the AI-generated outputs for each prompt variation and compare them to determine which variation was the most effective at producing the desired results. Take note of any patterns or trends that emerge from the comparison.

Refine your hypothesis and iterate:

Based on your findings, refine your initial hypothesis and repeat the systematic prompt exploration process. Continue iterating until you have identified the most effective prompt for your specific use case.

Systematic prompt exploration is a crucial technique that can lead to the discovery of new insights into how the AI model operates when presented with various prompts. This technique can also help you develop a deeper understanding of the most effective strategies for the specific tasks you are trying to accomplish.

By employing this advanced technique, you can further hone your prompt engineering skills and generate even higher-quality AI outputs. Additionally, engaging in systematic prompt exploration can also help you identify potential areas for improvement in your AI model and prompt engineering process, allowing you to continuously refine and optimize your approach. Overall, incorporating systematic prompt exploration into your AI development toolkit can have a significant impact on the quality and effectiveness of your AI outputs.

6.2 Leveraging Model-generated Suggestions

One advanced prompt engineering strategy involves leveraging the AI model's ability to generate suggestions or recommendations as part of the prompt itself. This can help guide the model towards generating more relevant and useful outputs.

To use model-generated suggestions effectively, follow these guidelines:

Design a dynamic prompt:

Create a prompt that includes the AI model's suggestions as part of the input. You can achieve this by using a two-step process: First, generate suggestions using the AI model; then, incorporate those suggestions into the prompt for the main task.

Example: For a content recommendation system, you can first use the AI to generate a list of potential topics based on user interests. Then, include this list in the prompt to request a more detailed content plan.

- Step 1: "Generate a list of 5 interesting topics based on the user's interest in technology, science, and environment."
- Step 2: "Using the following topics [insert AI-generated topic list], create a detailed content plan for a weekly newsletter."

Encourage creativity and diversity:

When designing a prompt that incorporates model-generated suggestions, make sure to leave room for creativity and diversity. Avoid overly constraining the AI model, which may limit its ability to generate novel and valuable outputs.

Example: Instead of asking the AI model to generate content based on specific suggestions, ask it to use those suggestions as inspiration or starting points for generating more diverse ideas.

Evaluate and refine suggestions:

Assess the quality of the model-generated suggestions and refine them as needed. You can iterate on the AI-generated suggestions to improve their relevance and usefulness before incorporating them into the main prompt.

Combine suggestions with other strategies:

You can combine the use of model-generated suggestions with other prompt engineering strategies, such as context-setting, providing explicit instructions, or employing a conversational approach, to further enhance the AI-generated outputs.

By leveraging model-generated suggestions, you can guide the AI model towards generating more relevant and useful outputs for your specific tasks. This advanced prompt engineering strategy can help you achieve better results and unlock the full potential of AI models. To elaborate further, consider the following:

When using model-generated suggestions, you can input specific keywords or phrases that will prompt the AI model to generate outputs that are tailored to your needs, whether it's for data analysis, language processing, image recognition, or any other task that involves AI models. By doing so, you can ensure that the generated outputs are more accurate and useful, as they are specifically designed to meet your requirements.

Moreover, this strategy can also improve the performance of the AI model over time, as it learns from the suggested prompts and adapts to generate even better outputs. By continually refining the prompts, you can unlock the full potential of the AI model and achieve results that were previously thought impossible.

Therefore, leveraging model-generated suggestions as part of your AI workflow can be a game-changer, enabling you to achieve better results, increase efficiency, and gain a competitive edge in your industry. So why not give it a try and see what the power of prompt engineering can do for you?

6.3 Prompt Engineering for Multi-Task Learning

Multi-task learning involves training an AI model to perform multiple tasks simultaneously or sequentially. It can help improve the model's performance across tasks by allowing it to learn shared representations and transfer knowledge between tasks. In this section, we'll discuss how to engineer prompts effectively for multi-task learning scenarios.

Define related tasks:

Start by identifying multiple tasks that are related in some way, either through shared inputs, outputs, or underlying concepts. The tasks should be complementary and have the potential to benefit from shared learning.

Example: If you want to create a comprehensive report on a company, you could define tasks like summarizing financial data, extracting key performance indicators, analyzing market trends, and generating a SWOT analysis.

Design interdependent prompts:

Create prompts that reflect the interdependence of the tasks and encourage the AI model to transfer knowledge between them. You can do this by providing context from one task to another or by chaining prompts together in a sequence.

Example: For the company report, you could first prompt the AI model to summarize financial data and then ask it to analyze market trends based on the financial summary.

Encourage shared learning:

In your prompts, emphasize the connections between tasks and encourage the AI model to draw upon its knowledge of one task when working on another.

Example: When asking the AI model to generate a SWOT analysis, encourage it to consider the financial data and market trends it has already analyzed.

Evaluate performance across tasks:

Assess the AI model's performance on each task individually and in combination with other tasks. This can help you determine whether the model is effectively transferring knowledge between tasks and identify areas for improvement.

Iterate and refine prompts:

Based on your evaluation, refine the prompts and their interdependencies to improve the AI model's multi-task learning performance. You may need to adjust the prompts' structure, sequence, or level of detail to achieve better results.

By carefully engineering prompts for multi-task learning, you can help the AI model learn shared representations and transfer knowledge between tasks, leading to better performance across a range of related tasks. This advanced prompt engineering strategy can unlock new capabilities and improve the efficiency of AI models in complex problem-solving scenarios.

Moreover, by utilizing multi-task learning, the AI model can gain a more comprehensive understanding of the data and develop a more nuanced representation. This can enable the model to make more accurate judgments and predictions, and ultimately lead to better outcomes. Additionally, the use of advanced prompt engineering strategies can help to mitigate the issue of catastrophic forgetting, allowing the model to retain previously learned information and build upon it over time. By incorporating these techniques into the development and training of AI models, we can continue to push the boundaries of what is possible in complex problem-solving scenarios.

6.4 Adversarial Prompt Engineering

Adversarial prompt engineering is an advanced strategy that involves crafting prompts to intentionally challenge the AI model's capabilities, expose its weaknesses, and improve its performance. It can help you gain a deeper understanding of the model's limitations and build more robust AI applications.

Here are some techniques for effective adversarial prompt engineering:

Identify potential weaknesses:

Start by pinpointing areas where the AI model may have difficulties, such as handling ambiguous or complex inputs, dealing with rare or out-of-distribution data, or maintaining consistency across multiple outputs.

Example: If you are working with a text summarization model, you may want to explore how it handles lengthy or poorly structured inputs.

Craft challenging prompts:

Create prompts that are designed to challenge the AI model in the identified areas of weakness. These prompts should be difficult but not impossible for the model to handle, so that you can assess its performance and identify areas for improvement.

Example: For the text summarization model, you could create a prompt asking it to summarize a long and convoluted article, or an article with multiple conflicting viewpoints.

Evaluate model performance:

Assess the AI model's performance on the adversarial prompts, paying close attention to errors, inconsistencies, or undesirable outputs. This evaluation can reveal insights into the model's limitations and potential areas for improvement.

Adjust model settings and training:

Based on your evaluation, you may need to adjust the AI model's settings or training data to address its weaknesses. You can also use the insights gained from adversarial prompt engineering to inform the development of more robust AI models.

Example: If the text summarization model struggles with long and convoluted articles, you may need to adjust its settings to handle longer inputs or provide additional training data that includes similar examples.

Iterate and refine prompts:

Continue iterating on your adversarial prompts, adjusting them as needed to challenge the AI model further and assess its performance improvements over time.

Adversarial prompt engineering is a complex and sophisticated technique that can provide valuable insights into the limitations of an AI model. By using this advanced strategy, you can explore the boundaries of your AI model's capabilities and identify areas where it needs improvement. This can help you build more robust AI applications that can perform well even in challenging scenarios.

Additionally, adversarial prompt engineering can help you ensure that your AI model is better equipped to handle real-world challenges. By testing your model's performance in a variety of scenarios, you can identify potential weaknesses and make targeted improvements to strengthen its overall performance. This can be particularly valuable for applications that require high levels of accuracy and precision, such as medical diagnosis or financial analysis.

Overall, the use of adversarial prompt engineering can be an important tool for developers seeking to build more advanced and effective AI applications. By leveraging this sophisticated technique, you can gain a deeper understanding of your model's capabilities and limitations, and work to improve its performance in a variety of challenging scenarios.

6.5 Leveraging Auxiliary Tasks for Prompt Engineering

Auxiliary tasks are supplementary tasks that are not the primary focus of an AI model but can help improve its performance on the main task by providing additional learning signals. In this section, we'll discuss how to leverage auxiliary tasks in prompt engineering to enhance the AI model's capabilities.

Identify related auxiliary tasks:

Start by identifying auxiliary tasks that are related to the main task and can provide valuable learning signals. These tasks should complement the main task and help the AI model learn useful features or representations.

Example: If your main task is sentiment analysis, an auxiliary task could be part-of-speech tagging or named entity recognition, which can help the model better understand the structure and content of the text.

Create prompts for auxiliary tasks:

Develop prompts for the auxiliary tasks that encourage the AI model to learn relevant features or representations for the main task. The prompts should be designed to focus on aspects of the auxiliary tasks that are most relevant to the main task.

Example: For part-of-speech tagging as an auxiliary task, you could create prompts that ask the AI model to identify the parts of speech for words in sentences with strong sentiment, like "The service at this restaurant was absolutely terrible!"

Train the AI model on auxiliary tasks:

One potential method for improving the performance of AI models is to integrate auxiliary task prompts into the training process. This can be achieved through either training the model on the auxiliary tasks simultaneously with the main task (also known as multi-task learning) or by pre-training the model on the auxiliary tasks before fine-tuning it on the main task. By incorporating these auxiliary tasks, the AI model is able to learn additional features and patterns that can further enhance its ability to perform the main task.

This can result in a more robust and accurate model, as well as potentially opening up new avenues for research and development in the field of AI. Therefore, it is crucial for researchers and practitioners to consider incorporating auxiliary tasks into their AI model training process.

Evaluate the AI model's performance:

To thoroughly evaluate the performance of an AI model, it is essential to assess its performance not only on the main task but also on the auxiliary tasks. By doing so, you can gain a more comprehensive understanding of how the model is functioning and determine whether the auxiliary tasks are contributing positively to its performance.

Furthermore, analyzing the performance of the model on the auxiliary tasks can help identify areas for improvement. For example, if the model is performing poorly on a particular auxiliary task, it may be an indication that the model requires additional training in that area.

Therefore, it is highly recommended to assess the AI model's performance on both the main task and the auxiliary tasks to obtain a more complete picture of its capabilities and potential areas for improvement.

Iterate and refine auxiliary tasks:

Based on your evaluation, refine the auxiliary tasks and their prompts to improve the AI model's performance on the main task. You may need to adjust the focus or difficulty of the auxiliary tasks or explore additional auxiliary tasks to achieve better results.

By leveraging auxiliary tasks in prompt engineering, you can provide the AI model with additional learning signals that help it learn more robust features and representations, leading to better performance on the main task. This advanced strategy not only benefits the model's performance in the main task, but can also be useful in improving its performance in a variety of scenarios, including challenging ones. For example, auxiliary tasks can help the model handle noisy data better, and can also help it learn more about the relationships between different features in the data.

Furthermore, by providing the model with a wider range of learning signals, you can help it learn more complex patterns and structures in the data, which can lead to even more accurate predictions and classifications. So, if you are looking to enhance the capabilities of your AI model and improve its performance, leveraging auxiliary tasks in prompt engineering is definitely a strategy worth exploring.

CHAPTER 7: Real-world Applications and Use Cases

Prompt engineering has emerged as a powerful technique to harness the capabilities of AI language models across a wide range of real-world applications and use cases. In this chapter, we will explore some of the most common and impactful applications of prompt engineering, demonstrating how it can be employed to achieve better results in various industries and domains. We will cover content generation and editing, customer service, marketing and advertising, data extraction and analysis, and more. Through these use cases, you'll gain a deeper understanding of the practical implications of prompt engineering and how it can be tailored to address specific challenges and objectives.

7.1 Content Generation and Editing

In this chapter, we will explore various real-world applications and use cases of prompt engineering. The first topic we will discuss is content generation and editing, which encompasses a wide range of applications, from blog post creation to social media content and beyond. As AI language models become more advanced, prompt engineering plays a crucial role in harnessing their power to generate and edit high-quality content efficiently.

Content Generation:

1. Blog posts and articles: By crafting prompts that specify the topic, target audience, and desired format of a blog post or

article, you can use AI models to generate content drafts. For example, you could create a prompt like "Write a 1000-word blog post for a beginner audience on the topic of gardening tips for small spaces."

2. Social media content: You can use prompt engineering to generate engaging social media content, such as tweets, Facebook posts, or LinkedIn updates. For example, a prompt could be "Create an engaging tweet that promotes our new gardening tool designed for small spaces."

3. Product descriptions: AI models can help create compelling product descriptions for e-commerce websites or marketing materials. A prompt might look like "Write a 150-word product description for a compact, foldable gardening shovel targeted at urban dwellers."

Content Editing:

1. Grammar and style checking: AI models can be used to identify grammar and style issues in text and provide suggestions for improvement. For example, you can create a prompt like "Identify and correct any grammar and style issues in the following paragraph: 'Gardening is a enjoyable hobby. Theirs many benefits to growing plants in small places.'"

2. Rewriting and paraphrasing: If you need to rewrite or paraphrase content for clarity or to avoid plagiarism, you can use prompt engineering to guide the AI model. For example, a prompt could be "Rewrite the following sentence in a more concise and clear manner: 'Gardening is a great way for people to connect with nature and enjoy the outdoors, even if they only have a small amount of space available.'"

3. Content optimization: AI models can help optimize content for specific purposes or platforms, such as search engine optimization (SEO) or email marketing. For example, a prompt might look like "Optimize the following blog post title for SEO: 'Gardening Tips for People with Limited Space.'"

By utilizing the latest prompt engineering techniques in content generation and editing applications, you can take advantage of the tremendous potential afforded by AI models to create, refine, and optimize high-quality content quickly, easily, and cost-effectively. This not only enables you to save time and resources, but also frees up your valuable energy and attention to focus on other important aspects of your business or project, such as marketing, customer engagement, and strategic planning.

Whether you are a small startup or a large enterprise, prompt engineering can help you streamline your content production process, enhance your brand image, and stay ahead of the competition in today's fast-paced digital landscape.

Practical Examples

Example 1: Generating a blog post introduction Prompt: "Write an engaging introduction for a blog post about the health benefits of yoga." Model output: "Yoga, an ancient practice that has been transforming lives for thousands of years, offers more than just flexibility and balance. With a myriad of health benefits waiting to be unlocked, yoga is a treasure trove for holistic well-being. In this blog post, we will delve into the numerous ways yoga can enhance your physical, mental, and emotional health, revealing why this timeless practice should be an integral part of your wellness routine."

Example 2: Summarizing a news article Prompt: "Summarize the main points of the following news article in 3 sentences: [insert news article]." Model output: "Tech giant XYZ announced its latest flagship smartphone today, featuring an innovative 3D camera and a new AI-powered virtual assistant. The device will be available for pre-order next week and is expected to hit the shelves in early June. Analysts predict strong sales, as the phone's features and competitive pricing are likely to appeal to a wide range of consumers."

Example 3: Generating a catchy marketing slogan Prompt: "Create a catchy slogan for a new eco-friendly cleaning product line." Model output: "Clean and Green: Sparkling Results, Earth-Friendly Solutions."

Example 4: Expanding a bullet point into a paragraph Prompt: "Expand the following bullet point into a detailed paragraph: 'Benefits of remote work: Increased productivity.'" Model output: "One of the most significant benefits of remote work is the potential for increased productivity. When employees have the flexibility to work from the comfort of their homes, they can create a personalized environment that caters to their individual work styles and preferences. Without the distractions and interruptions commonly found in traditional office settings, remote workers can focus more intently on their tasks. Additionally, the time saved from daily commuting can be redirected towards work, further enhancing overall productivity."

Example 5: Proofreading and editing a paragraph Prompt: "Proofread and edit the following paragraph: 'The affects of climate change are far-reatching and impacts many aspects of our live's. From rising sea levels, to more frequent storms and wildfires, the consequences are becoming more seveer and unpredictable.'" Model output: "The effects of climate change are far-reaching and impact many aspects of our lives. From rising sea levels to more frequent storms and wildfires, the consequences are becoming more severe and unpredictable."

These examples showcase how prompt engineering can be used to generate various types of content, summarize information, create slogans, expand ideas, and proofread and edit texts.

7.2 Question Answering and Information Retrieval

In this topic, we will discuss the application of prompt engineering in question answering and information retrieval systems. These systems are crucial in today's data-centric world, where large amounts of data are generated every day. The amount of data generated can make it difficult for users to find specific information they need, and this is where question answering and information retrieval systems come in. By using these systems, users can quickly and easily locate the information they need, saving them time and effort.

However, the accuracy and relevance of the responses provided by these systems are critical. This is where prompt engineering comes in. AI language models can be guided to provide more accurate and relevant responses to user queries by using prompt engineering techniques. By fine-tuning the language models to specific prompts, the models can be made to produce more accurate and relevant responses. Therefore, prompt engineering is an essential aspect of question answering and information retrieval systems, and it is crucial to understand its application in these systems.

Question Answering:

1. Fact-based questions: By creating prompts that explicitly request factual information, you can guide AI models to provide accurate answers. For example, a prompt like "What is the capital city of France?" should yield the correct response: "Paris."
2. How-to questions: You can use prompt engineering to obtain step-by-step instructions or guidance on various tasks. For example, a prompt might be "Explain how to change a flat tire on a bicycle."
3. Contextual questions: AI models can be guided to provide answers that take context into account, such as specific timeframes or situations. For example, a prompt could be "What were the main causes of World War II?"

Information Retrieval:

1. Keyword-based search: You can use prompts that include specific keywords to guide the AI model in extracting relevant information from a text source. For example, a prompt like "Find three main points about climate change from the following article: [insert article text]" can help retrieve pertinent details.
2. Summarization: AI models can be guided to generate summaries of lengthy texts or documents, enabling users to quickly grasp the main ideas. For example, a prompt might be "Summarize the key findings of the following research paper: [insert paper text]."
3. Multi-document information synthesis: AI models can be used to synthesize information from multiple documents, providing a comprehensive response to user queries. For example, a prompt could be "Compare the benefits and

drawbacks of solar power and wind power based on the following sources: [insert source texts]."

By utilizing prompt engineering techniques in question answering and information retrieval systems, you can enhance the performance of AI models in generating more accurate and relevant responses. Prompt engineering involves designing and optimizing prompts that allow the model to better understand the users' queries and provide more informative responses. This can be achieved by analyzing the patterns and commonalities in the users' queries, and identifying the key information that the model should focus on.

By doing so, users can obtain more insightful and precise answers to their questions, which can improve the efficiency and effectiveness of the overall search experience. Additionally, prompt engineering can also help to mitigate the impact of biases and inaccuracies in the underlying data, which can further enhance the reliability and trustworthiness of the responses generated by the AI model.

Practical Examples

Example 1: Answering a trivia question Prompt: "Who is the author of the Harry Potter series?" Model output: "The author of the Harry Potter series is J.K. Rowling."

Example 2: Finding a solution to a math problem Prompt: "What is the solution to the quadratic equation $x^2 - 5x + 6 = 0$?" Model output: "The solutions to the quadratic equation $x^2 - 5x + 6 = 0$ are $x = 2$ and $x = 3$."

Example 3: Providing historical context Prompt: "What were the main causes of World War I?" Model output: "The main causes of World War I were a complex mix of factors, including militarism, alliances, imperialism, and nationalism. The immediate trigger, however, was the assassination of Archduke Franz Ferdinand of Austria by a Serbian nationalist in June 1914."

Example 4: Retrieving information from a given text Prompt: "According to the following text, when did the company launch its new product? 'XYZ Company unveiled its latest product on January 12, 2023, marking a significant milestone in the company's journey to revolutionize the industry.'" Model output: "According to the given text, the company launched its new product on January 12, 2023."

Example 5: Answering a health-related question Prompt: "What are the common symptoms of the flu?" Model output: "Common symptoms of the flu include fever, chills, muscle aches, cough, congestion, runny nose, headaches, and fatigue. Some individuals may also experience vomiting and diarrhea, though these symptoms are more common in children than adults."

These examples illustrate how prompt engineering can be utilized to answer a wide range of questions and retrieve specific information from provided texts.

7.3 Language Translation and Interpretation

In this topic, we will delve deeper into the fascinating world of prompt engineering for language translation and interpretation tasks. As the use of AI language models becomes more widespread, the need for accurate translations between different languages becomes increasingly important for global communication across cultures and industries. While these models have made significant strides in recent years, prompt engineering can further enhance their performance by providing more specific and tailored guidance for different types of translations and interpretations.

By creating targeted prompts that help the models better understand the nuances of different languages and dialects, we can improve their accuracy and effectiveness in a range of real-world scenarios. So let's explore the exciting possibilities of prompt engineering and how it can revolutionize the way we communicate across borders and cultures!

Language Translation:

1. Context-aware translation: Using prompts that provide context can help AI models generate more accurate translations. For example, you can specify the subject matter or domain to improve the translation's accuracy: "Translate the following medical text from English to French: [insert text]."
2. Idiomatic expressions: AI models can struggle with idiomatic expressions that don't have direct translations. Prompt engineering can guide the model to provide a more accurate translation by providing context or asking for a paraphrase. For example: "Translate the following English idiom to Spanish, keeping the meaning intact: 'The ball is in your court.'"
3. Formality and tone: You can use prompt engineering to adjust the formality and tone of a translation. For example, you might request a formal translation: "Translate the following English text to Japanese using formal language: [insert text]."

Language Interpretation:

1. Paraphrasing: AI models can be used to rephrase text in the same language, providing a clearer or simpler version. Prompts can guide the model to produce an interpretation that maintains the original meaning while using different words: "Paraphrase the following sentence while preserving its meaning: 'The examination of the evidence led the investigator to the inescapable conclusion.'"
2. Text simplification: AI models can simplify complex text, making it more accessible to a wider audience. You can use prompts to guide the model to rewrite text at a lower reading level: "Simplify the following paragraph to a 5th-grade reading level: [insert text]."
3. Cultural adaptation: Prompt engineering can help AI models adapt content to make it more culturally appropriate or relevant for a specific audience. For example: "Adapt the following American recipe for a British audience: [insert recipe]."

By utilizing prompt engineering in language translation and interpretation tasks, AI models can provide more accurate translations, better handle idiomatic expressions, and adapt content to different cultural contexts. This can significantly improve the quality of communication between speakers of different languages and make information more accessible to diverse audiences.

Moreover, AI models can also help overcome the language barriers that exist in many industries, such as healthcare, finance, and marketing. For instance, in the healthcare industry, AI-powered translation tools can be used to help doctors and nurses communicate with patients who speak different languages. This can improve the accuracy of medical diagnoses and reduce the risk of miscommunication. Similarly, in the finance industry, AI models can be used to translate financial documents for clients who speak different languages, making it easier for them to understand the terms and conditions of their investments. In the marketing industry, AI models can be used to translate advertising campaigns and product descriptions for global audiences, opening up new markets and increasing sales.

In addition, prompt engineering can also help AI models to better understand the nuances of different languages and dialects, allowing them to provide more accurate translations and interpretations. This is particularly important in regions where multiple languages and dialects are spoken, such as India and Africa. By improving the accuracy of translations and interpretations, prompt engineering can help to bridge the language gap and promote greater understanding and cooperation between different cultures and communities.

Practical Examples

Example 1: English to Spanish translation Prompt: "Translate the following English sentence to Spanish: 'Hello, how are you?'" Model output: "Hola, ¿cómo estás?"

Example 2: French to English translation Prompt: "Translate the following French sentence to English: 'Le chat est sur la table.'" Model output: "The cat is on the table."

Example 3: Chinese to English translation Prompt: "Translate the following Chinese sentence to English: '你好吗？'" Model output: "How are you?"

Example 4: English to German translation Prompt: "Translate the following English sentence to German: 'I love to travel and explore new places.'" Model output: "Ich liebe es zu reisen und neue Orte zu erkunden."

Example 5: Russian to English translation Prompt: "Translate the following Russian sentence to English: 'Какие планы на выходные?'" Model output: "What are your plans for the weekend?"

These examples showcase how prompt engineering can be used to translate text between various languages and facilitate understanding across different cultures and linguistic backgrounds.

7.4 Sentiment Analysis and Text Classification

In this topic, we will discuss the fascinating and rapidly evolving field of prompt engineering in sentiment analysis and text classification tasks. Prompt engineering is a technique used to improve the performance of AI language models for these tasks, and it involves the careful selection and tuning of prompts, which are small pieces of text used to guide the model's response. By using prompts, we can enhance the model's understanding of the context and improve its ability to accurately identify sentiment and classify text.

Sentiment analysis, as mentioned earlier, involves determining the sentiment or emotion expressed in a piece of text. This is an important task in a wide range of applications, from social media monitoring to market research. With the explosion of social media and the increasing importance of customer feedback, sentiment analysis has become a critical tool for businesses looking to enhance their customer experience and improve their reputation.

Text classification, on the other hand, is the process of assigning predefined categories or labels to text. This can be useful in a variety of settings, such as filtering spam emails, identifying topics in news articles, and detecting fake news. By using AI language models to perform text classification, we can automate this process and save time and resources.

Overall, the combination of AI language models and prompt engineering has tremendous potential for improving the accuracy and efficiency of sentiment analysis and text classification tasks. As the field continues to evolve, we can expect to see even more innovative approaches and techniques emerge that will further enhance the capabilities of these powerful tools.

Sentiment Analysis:

1. Binary sentiment analysis: By crafting prompts that ask for a binary sentiment classification, you can guide AI models to identify whether a given text expresses a positive or negative sentiment. For example: "Determine the sentiment of the following review as positive or negative: [insert review]."
2. Emotion classification: AI models can be guided to identify specific emotions expressed in a text. For example, a prompt could be "Classify the emotion expressed in the following text as one of the following: joy, sadness, anger, or fear: [insert text]."
3. Aspect-based sentiment analysis: With prompt engineering, AI models can analyze the sentiment towards specific aspects within a piece of text. For example: "Identify the sentiment towards the product's design and customer service in the following review: [insert review]."

Text Classification:

1. Topic categorization: AI models can be guided to classify texts into predefined topics or categories. For example, a prompt might be "Classify the following article into one of these categories: technology, sports, politics, or entertainment: [insert article]."

2. Spam detection: You can use prompts to guide AI models in identifying spam messages or emails. For example: "Determine whether the following email is spam or legitimate: [insert email]."
3. Intent classification: AI models can be guided to classify user inputs according to their underlying intent, which is particularly useful for chatbots and virtual assistants. For example: "Classify the following user input as a request for information, a complaint, or a suggestion: [insert user input]."

By applying prompt engineering to sentiment analysis and text classification tasks, you can greatly enhance the performance of AI language models when identifying the sentiments and emotions conveyed in text, as well as when classifying such text into predefined categories. This can be useful across a wide variety of domains, including customer service, marketing, content management, and more.

In recent years, the use of AI language models has become increasingly prevalent across a broad range of industries. However, these models often struggle when it comes to accurately identifying the sentiment and emotional tone of text, as well as accurately classifying it into predefined categories based on its content. By utilizing prompt engineering methods, we can help these models to better understand the nuances of language, and to more accurately capture the sentiment and emotions being expressed in any given text. This can have significant benefits in a variety of settings, from improving customer service interactions to enhancing the effectiveness of marketing campaigns and other content management efforts.

Practical Exercises

Example 1: Analyzing sentiment of a movie review Prompt: "Determine the sentiment of the following movie review: 'The film was absolutely stunning, with breathtaking visuals and a captivating storyline that kept me on the edge of my seat.'" Model output: "Positive"

Example 2: Classifying a support ticket Prompt: "Categorize the following support ticket: 'I am unable to log in to my account. I've tried resetting my password, but it still doesn't work.'" Model output: "Login Issues"

Example 3: Identifying spam emails Prompt: "Is the following email spam or not? 'Congratulations! You've won a $1,000 gift card. Click on the link below to claim your prize.'" Model output: "Spam"

Example 4: Analyzing the sentiment of a product review Prompt: "Determine the sentiment of the following product review: 'The headphones were extremely uncomfortable and the sound quality was terrible. I wouldn't recommend them to anyone.'" Model output: "Negative"

Example 5: Classifying news articles Prompt: "Categorize the following news headline: 'New breakthrough in cancer research brings hope to millions of patients.'" Model output: "Health"

These examples illustrate how prompt engineering can be used to analyze sentiment and classify text into various categories for a wide range of applications.

CHAPTER 8: Ethical Considerations in Prompt Engineering

In this chapter, we will explore the ethical considerations that are crucial when working with language models and prompt engineering. One of the key things to keep in mind is the potential for biases to be introduced into the training data or the model itself, which can have serious consequences in the real world.

For example, if a language model is trained on data that is not representative of the diversity of human language, it may produce biased or discriminatory outputs. Similarly, privacy concerns can arise when sensitive data is used to train or deploy AI-based solutions, or when such solutions are used to make decisions that affect people's lives. It is important to address these ethical issues in order to create more inclusive, fair, and responsible AI applications that benefit everyone. Another consideration is how to ensure that the benefits of AI are distributed fairly across different groups and that no one is left behind in the quest for technological progress.

This may involve partnering with diverse communities to ensure that their needs and perspectives are incorporated into the development process, as well as developing policies and frameworks that promote equitable access to AI-based solutions. By taking these steps, we can create a more just and equitable society that harnesses the power of AI for the greater good.

8.1: Addressing Bias and Discrimination

Biases in language models can lead to unfair and discriminatory outcomes. These biases may result from the training data containing historical and societal biases. As a prompt engineer, it is essential to be aware of these issues and take steps to mitigate them.

Recognize potential biases:

When creating prompts, be mindful of possible biases in the language model's responses. This awareness can help you design prompts that minimize biased outcomes.

Example: If you ask a model to generate a list of successful people in a certain field, it may produce a list that disproportionately represents a specific gender or ethnicity. Recognizing this potential bias, you can reframe the prompt to encourage a more diverse and inclusive list of people.

Design inclusive prompts:

Write prompts that encourage fairness and inclusivity. Consider incorporating words or phrases that signal the importance of diversity and equality.

Example: Instead of asking the model to generate a list of "great leaders," you could prompt it with "great leaders from diverse backgrounds and communities."

Test and iterate:

Regularly test your prompts for biased outcomes, and iterate on your prompt designs to reduce any detected biases. Continuously evaluating and refining your prompts will help ensure more ethical results.

Example: After generating a list of successful people, check if the list includes a diverse representation of individuals across genders, ethnicities, and other demographics. If not, adjust the prompt and retest to strive for a more balanced outcome.

Collaborate with diverse teams:

Work with teams composed of diverse perspectives and backgrounds to better identify and address potential biases. Different perspectives can provide valuable insights into potential blind spots in your prompt engineering process.

By taking these steps, you can work towards creating more ethically responsible AI systems that address bias and discrimination, leading to more equitable outcomes for all users. One way to start this process is by analyzing the data used to train these AI models. This can help identify any biases or discriminatory patterns that may exist in the data, allowing developers to take steps to address these issues.

Additionally, implementing diverse teams and perspectives in the development process can also help to mitigate these issues. By bringing together individuals with different backgrounds and experiences, AI systems can be developed with a more comprehensive understanding of the various factors that may impact their users. Finally, ongoing evaluation and monitoring of these AI systems can help to ensure that they are functioning in a fair and equitable manner, and that any issues that arise are addressed in a timely and effective manner.

Practical Examples

Example 1: Original Prompt: "List the most successful scientists in history." Improved Prompt: "List successful scientists from various backgrounds and time periods in history."

Example 2: Original Prompt: "Describe the characteristics of a good CEO." Improved Prompt: "Describe the characteristics of a good CEO, considering diverse leadership styles and backgrounds."

Example 3: Original Prompt: "Generate a story about a group of friends who are software engineers at a tech company." Improved

Prompt: "Generate a story about a diverse group of friends with different genders, ethnicities, and backgrounds, who are software engineers at a tech company."

Example 4: Original Prompt: "Suggest the top 10 books for entrepreneurs to read." Improved Prompt: "Suggest the top 10 books for entrepreneurs to read, written by authors with diverse backgrounds and perspectives."

Example 5: Original Prompt: "Write an article about the most influential artists of the 20th century." Improved Prompt: "Write an article about the most influential artists of the 20th century, highlighting individuals from various cultural backgrounds and artistic movements."

These examples showcase how you can adjust prompts to encourage more diverse and inclusive results, helping to address potential biases and create more ethically responsible AI applications.

8.2: Privacy and Data Protection

Privacy and data protection are critical ethical considerations when working with language models and prompt engineering. Sensitive information, personal data, and potential privacy breaches can lead to unintended consequences and harm individuals or organizations. As a prompt engineer, it is essential to be aware of these concerns and take steps to protect privacy and data.

Anonymize data:

When working with real-world data, ensure that any personally identifiable information (PII) is anonymized or removed. This can help protect users' privacy and prevent the inadvertent sharing of sensitive information.

Example: If you're using customer reviews to train a model, remove names, email addresses, and other PII from the data before incorporating it into the training set.

Limit sensitive content:

Be cautious when designing prompts that could potentially lead to the generation of sensitive or harmful content. Set clear boundaries and guidelines for the model to follow to avoid violating users' privacy or generating inappropriate responses.

Example: If you're creating a prompt for a customer support chatbot, design the prompt to avoid asking for sensitive information, such as Social Security numbers or credit card details.

Implement safety mechanisms:

Employ safety mechanisms, such as content filters or moderation tools, to prevent the model from generating responses that could expose private information or harm users.

Example: Implement a content filter to detect and block the sharing of PII or offensive content in the model's generated responses.

Be transparent with users:

Inform users about how their data is used, stored, and protected, as well as any potential risks associated with using AI-generated content. This transparency can help build trust and promote responsible AI use.

Example: Create a clear privacy policy that outlines how user data is handled, including data retention and sharing practices, and provide a user-friendly explanation of the AI system's capabilities and limitations.

Comply with regulations:

Ensure that your prompt engineering practices comply with relevant data protection laws and regulations, such as the General Data Protection Regulation (GDPR) in the European Union or the California Consumer Privacy Act (CCPA) in the United States.

By considering these aspects of privacy and data protection, you can contribute to the development of more responsible, ethical AI applications that respect users' rights and protect their sensitive information. For instance, you can conduct a thorough analysis of the potential risks and benefits of the AI application you are developing, and ensure that the data you are using is accurate and up-to-date.

You can also implement appropriate security measures, such as encryption, to safeguard users' data from unauthorized access or theft. Furthermore, you can provide clear and transparent information to users about how their data will be used and who will have access to it. By doing so, you can build trust with your users and foster a culture of responsible data use in the development of AI applications.

Practical Examples

1. **Anonymizing Customer Feedback**: A company collects customer feedback to train an AI model that generates responses for their support chatbot. Before using the data, the company removes names, addresses, phone numbers, and any other personally identifiable information from the feedback, ensuring the privacy of their customers is protected.
2. **Health Chatbot with Privacy Limits**: A healthcare organization designs a chatbot to assist users with general health inquiries. To ensure privacy, the chatbot is designed with prompts that avoid asking for sensitive information, such as medical history or personal identification numbers. The chatbot is also programmed to provide general advice and encourage users to consult a medical professional for personalized guidance.
3. **Filtering PII in AI-generated Content**: An AI-based platform is used to generate personalized marketing emails. The company implements a content filter that automatically detects and blocks any personally identifiable information, such as email addresses or phone numbers, from being included in the generated content, ensuring privacy and compliance with data protection regulations.

4. **Transparent AI-powered Job Board**: A job board uses an AI model to match job seekers with relevant job openings. The platform clearly informs users about how their data is used and stored, the AI model's limitations, and the measures taken to protect their privacy. This transparency helps build trust and ensures users are aware of potential risks.

5. **Compliant AI-driven Financial Advisor**: A financial advising platform uses AI to generate personalized investment recommendations. The platform ensures compliance with data protection regulations, such as GDPR and CCPA, by implementing data minimization techniques, obtaining user consent, and providing clear information on data usage and storage policies. The platform also uses encryption and other security measures to protect users' sensitive financial data.

These examples demonstrate various ways prompt engineering can address privacy and data protection concerns, ensuring that AI applications are both useful and ethically responsible.

8.3: Transparency and Accountability

Transparency and accountability are critical in ethical AI and prompt engineering. In order to achieve transparency, developers must be open about the workings of an AI system, its limitations, and how it makes decisions. This openness extends to the data used to train the system, which should be publicly available whenever possible. Accountability, on the other hand, involves ensuring that those responsible for creating and deploying AI systems are held responsible for any consequences that arise from their use.

In addition to being ethical imperatives, transparency and accountability have practical benefits. For example, they can help build trust with users and stakeholders. When users understand how an AI system works and the limitations of its decision-making, they are more likely to trust it. Similarly, when stakeholders have confidence that those responsible for an AI system are being held accountable for its use, they are more likely to support the system's deployment.

In this section, we will delve deeper into the importance of transparency and accountability in prompt engineering. We will explore how these principles can be incorporated into AI applications and discuss the benefits that they can bring. By doing so, we hope to provide a comprehensive understanding of the role that transparency and accountability play in ethical AI and prompt engineering.

8.3.1 Importance of Transparency and Accountability:

Transparency is necessary for users to understand how an AI system works, its potential biases, and its limitations. This understanding helps build trust in AI applications and enables users to make informed decisions about their use. Accountability ensures that the developers, companies, and other stakeholders involved in creating and deploying AI systems are held responsible for any unintended consequences, promoting ethical development and usage.

8.3.2 Incorporating Transparency and Accountability in Prompt Engineering:

Here are some strategies to promote transparency and accountability in prompt engineering:

1. **Documentation and explainability**: Provide clear documentation that explains the design, development, and functioning of your AI system, including the data used for training and any biases that may exist.
2. **Openness about limitations**: Be candid about the limitations of your AI system, including areas where it may not perform well, to help users set realistic expectations and make informed decisions about its use.
3. **Regular audits and assessments**: Conduct periodic evaluations of your AI system to identify and mitigate any biases, inaccuracies, or unintended consequences that may emerge over time.
4. **Stakeholder involvement**: Engage with a diverse group of stakeholders, including users, experts, and potentially affected communities, to gather feedback and ensure that the AI system aligns with their needs and values.

5. **Responsible deployment**: Use AI systems only in contexts where they provide real value and do not cause undue harm. Monitor the performance of AI systems after deployment and be prepared to adjust or decommission them if necessary.

Examples

1. A news summarization AI is designed to generate summaries of articles from various sources. The developers provide clear documentation explaining how the AI was trained, its potential biases, and its limitations in understanding complex or nuanced language. They also include a feedback mechanism for users to report any issues, helping to improve the AI system over time.
2. An AI-driven hiring tool is used to screen job applicants. The company behind the tool discloses the factors it considers in its decision-making process and the limitations of the AI model in understanding the full context of an applicant's qualifications. They also establish an appeals process for applicants who believe they have been unfairly evaluated.
3. A city uses AI to optimize traffic light timings to reduce congestion. The city's government is transparent about the data used for training the AI system, its goals, and its limitations in handling unusual traffic situations. They also establish a process for residents to provide feedback on the system's performance and make any necessary adjustments.

By incorporating transparency and accountability into prompt engineering, developers can create AI systems that are more ethical, reliable, and trusted by users.

8.4: Responsible AI Deployment

Responsible AI deployment is a crucial aspect of the development of AI systems. The purpose of responsible AI deployment is to ensure that AI systems are implemented in a manner that is ethical, addresses potential risks, and creates positive outcomes for users and society. Therefore, it is important to understand the significance of responsible deployment and the strategies that can be used to ensure that AI systems are introduced in an ethically sound manner.

When implementing AI systems, it is essential to understand the potential risks that may arise from its use. For instance, AI systems may be susceptible to bias, which can lead to unfair treatment of certain groups of people. Therefore, it is important to take measures to mitigate these risks and ensure that AI systems are deployed in a responsible manner.

One strategy for ensuring responsible AI deployment is to involve a diverse group of stakeholders in the development and deployment process. This can include individuals from different backgrounds, such as ethicists, policy makers, and community representatives, who can provide different perspectives and insights on the ethical implications of AI systems.

Another strategy is to establish clear guidelines and standards for the development and deployment of AI systems. This can include ethical principles and codes of conduct that outline the responsibilities of developers and users of AI systems.

By implementing responsible AI deployment strategies, we can ensure that AI systems are introduced in an ethically sound manner, address potential risks, and create positive outcomes for users and society.

8.4.1 Importance of Responsible AI Deployment:

Deploying AI responsibly is crucial to ensuring that AI applications benefit users and society while minimizing potential harm. It also helps to build public trust in AI technologies, which is essential for their widespread adoption and success.

8.4.2 Strategies for Responsible AI Deployment:

Here are some strategies to promote responsible AI deployment:

1. Assess potential risks and benefits: Before deploying an AI system, carefully evaluate its potential impact on users, communities, and the environment. Consider both short-term and long-term consequences, and weigh the benefits against the risks.
2. Test and validate AI systems: Rigorously test your AI system in diverse, real-world scenarios to identify and address any flaws, biases, or unintended consequences before deployment.
3. Monitor and maintain AI systems post-deployment: Continuously monitor the performance and impact of your AI system after it has been deployed. Be prepared to adjust or decommission it if necessary to mitigate any harm or unintended consequences.
4. Establish a governance framework: Develop a clear governance structure for AI deployment that outlines roles, responsibilities, and decision-making processes. This framework should promote ethical practices, transparency, and accountability.
5. Engage stakeholders: Consult with a diverse group of stakeholders, including users, experts, and potentially affected communities, to gather feedback and ensure that your AI system aligns with their needs and values.

Examples

1. A healthcare organization deploys an AI system to help diagnose medical conditions. Before deployment, they conduct extensive testing and validation to ensure the system's accuracy and safety. They also provide training to medical professionals on the system's limitations and how to interpret its recommendations responsibly.
2. A financial institution uses AI-driven chatbots to assist customers with their queries. The institution conducts thorough risk assessments, evaluates the AI system's potential biases, and tests its performance across diverse customer demographics. They also establish a feedback mechanism for users to report any issues or concerns.
3. An AI-powered surveillance system is deployed by a city to enhance public safety. The city consults with local

communities and privacy experts to address potential concerns and minimize any negative impacts. They also implement strict data protection policies and provide transparent information on the system's functioning and goals.

By following these strategies, developers can deploy AI systems responsibly, ensuring that they contribute positively to users and society while minimizing potential harm.

CHAPTER 9: Future Trends and Challenges

The field of prompt engineering has experienced exponential growth and unprecedented innovation in recent years, and this trend is poised to continue. With the advent of increasingly powerful language models and the rapid pace of AI research, prompt engineering is becoming more complex and sophisticated. As we look to the future, it is critical to consider the challenges and opportunities that lie ahead, as they will shape the direction of prompt engineering and influence the strategies and techniques used to optimize human-AI interaction.

One of the most significant trends in prompt engineering is the emergence of new AI architectures. These architectures are designed to enable more efficient and effective processing of natural language data, and they have already shown promising results in a variety of applications. Another important trend is the growing focus on AI ethics, as the use of AI becomes more widespread and raises important questions about privacy, bias, and fairness.

In addition to these trends, there is also a growing demand for multilingual and multimodal solutions. As the world becomes more connected, the ability to communicate effectively across different languages and modes is becoming increasingly important. Prompt engineering is well-positioned to address these challenges, as it is uniquely suited to develop solutions that can bridge these divides.

By examining these topics and more, we aim to provide a comprehensive understanding of the future landscape of prompt engineering. Our goal is to enable practitioners to stay ahead of the curve and harness the potential of new developments in the field, so that they can continue to deliver innovative and impactful solutions that enhance human-AI interaction.

9.1 Emerging AI Architectures and Implications for Prompt Engineering

AI research and development are continuously advancing, leading to the emergence of new architectures and techniques. The potential impact of these developments on prompt engineering cannot be overstated. With the emergence of more efficient, accurate, and flexible language models, prompt engineering strategies can be significantly enhanced. In this topic, we will delve deeper into some of the most promising AI architectures and explore their potential implications for prompt engineering.

We will also examine how these new architectures and techniques can be harnessed to build more effective prompt engineering strategies, and how they can be used to optimize the performance of existing ones. Additionally, we will discuss the challenges associated with implementing these new architectures and techniques, and identify potential solutions to overcome them.

1. **Transformer-XL:** Transformer-XL extends the traditional Transformer architecture by introducing a novel mechanism called segment-level recurrence. This approach allows the model to learn long-range dependencies better, which can lead to improved context understanding and more coherent generated text in prompt engineering applications.
2. **Hybrid Models:** The integration of deep learning with other AI techniques, such as reinforcement learning or symbolic reasoning, could result in hybrid models that exhibit more advanced reasoning capabilities. These models may necessitate novel prompt engineering techniques that leverage their unique strengths.
3. **Sparse Transformer:** The Sparse Transformer architecture introduces sparsity into the attention mechanism of the traditional Transformer model. By doing so, it can efficiently

process long sequences without sacrificing performance, making it particularly suitable for tasks involving large-scale text generation and analysis.

4. **Capsule Networks**: Capsule Networks are a relatively new approach to deep learning that aims to better model hierarchical relationships between features. While primarily explored in the context of computer vision, Capsule Networks have the potential to impact natural language processing tasks, including prompt engineering, by enabling more effective representation and understanding of complex linguistic structures.

5. **Neuromorphic Computing**: Neuromorphic computing is an emerging field that seeks to develop AI systems inspired by the structure and function of the human brain. These systems have the potential to be more energy-efficient and capable of real-time learning, which could lead to prompt engineering applications that are faster, more adaptable, and less resource-intensive.

6. **Quantum Computing**: Quantum computing offers the promise of solving complex problems and processing large datasets much more quickly than traditional computing methods. As quantum computing becomes more accessible, it may enable significant advancements in AI and natural language processing, potentially revolutionizing the way prompt engineering is conducted.

7. **Dynamic and Adaptive Models**: Future AI models may be designed to dynamically adapt their architecture or behavior based on the input data or specific use case. Prompt engineering in this context may involve creating prompts that can guide the model's adaptation process effectively.

8. **Multimodal Models**: As AI moves towards incorporating different modalities, such as text, images, and audio, prompt engineering will need to evolve to handle these additional complexities. This could involve designing prompts that combine different types of input data or require models to produce outputs in multiple modalities.

As these emerging architectures become more prevalent, prompt engineers must keep themselves informed about the latest developments in order to adapt their approaches accordingly. They should pay attention to the latest research, attend conferences and seminars, and engage with the broader AI community. By doing so, they can stay up-to-date with the latest techniques and best practices, and ensure that they continue to create effective and efficient prompts that are tailored to the ever-evolving landscape of AI.

Additionally, they should seek out opportunities to collaborate with other experts in the field, whether through research partnerships or online forums. This can help them to gain new insights and perspectives, and to stay ahead of the curve in this rapidly-changing field.

9.2 Personalization and Adaptive Prompts

Personalization and adaptive prompts are an emerging trend in prompt engineering that focuses on tailoring prompts to individual users or specific situations. This approach can lead to more accurate and relevant responses from AI models, ultimately improving user experience and satisfaction. In this section, we will explore the concept of personalization and adaptive prompts and how they can be implemented in various applications.

9.2.1 User-specific Prompts

By considering user preferences, background, and prior interactions, personalized prompts can be crafted to better suit individual users. For instance, if a user frequently asks questions about technology news, a personalized prompt could prioritize tech-related responses when faced with ambiguous queries.

Example: A user who often discusses soccer may ask, "What are the latest updates?" A personalized prompt could guide the model to generate a response related to soccer news, even though the question itself is vague.

9.2.2 Context-aware Prompts

Adaptive prompts take into account the context in which the AI model is being used. For example, if an AI model is deployed within a customer support chatbot for a specific company, prompts can be designed to prioritize responses that are relevant to the company's products and services.

Example: A user asks, "How do I reset my password?" In the context of a specific company's support chatbot, an adaptive prompt could generate a response that outlines the password reset process for that particular company's website.

9.2.3 Dynamic Prompts

Dynamic prompts can be designed to change over time or based on external factors, such as real-time events or updated information. This allows the AI model to provide up-to-date and relevant responses.

Example: In a news summarization application, dynamic prompts could ensure that the AI model generates summaries based on the most recent news articles, even as new stories are published throughout the day.

9.2.4 Learning-based Prompts

By leveraging machine learning or reinforcement learning techniques, prompts can be optimized and adapted based on the AI model's performance and user feedback. This allows the prompts to improve over time, leading to better AI responses.

Example: An AI model that recommends movies could start with a generic prompt, but over time, as the user provides feedback on the recommendations, the prompt can be refined to better capture the user's preferences and generate more personalized movie suggestions.

9.2.5 Multimodal Personalization:

As AI models begin to handle multiple data modalities (e.g., text, images, audio), prompts can be personalized and adapted to incorporate different types of data to provide more accurate and relevant responses.

Example: In a language learning application, an adaptive prompt could provide personalized feedback to users by analyzing both their text input and spoken responses to identify common errors and suggest targeted improvements.

By incorporating personalization and adaptive prompts into prompt engineering, AI models can become more attuned to the specific needs of individual users and diverse contexts, ultimately providing more valuable and satisfying experiences.

This is particularly important as AI continues to play an increasingly prominent role in our daily lives. The ability for AI to adapt to individual users and contexts can greatly improve the overall usability and effectiveness of these systems. Furthermore, by providing more tailored experiences, AI can help to reduce frustration and improve engagement among users.

This can lead to higher levels of satisfaction and even increased productivity in certain contexts, such as in the workplace or in educational settings. Overall, the integration of personalization and adaptive prompts represents an important step forward in the development of more effective and user-friendly AI systems.

To further enhance the understanding of personalization and adaptive prompts, it's worth noting that developing these types of prompts may come with some challenges:

1. **Balancing personalization and privacy**: While personalized prompts can improve user experience, it's crucial to handle user data responsibly and ensure privacy is maintained. Implementing techniques such as data anonymization, secure storage, and data usage policies can help strike the right balance.
2. **Computational complexity**: Adapting prompts in real-time or continually learning from user interactions can increase the computational requirements of AI models. Efficient algorithms and prompt optimization techniques should be

employed to minimize the computational burden while maintaining prompt effectiveness.

3. **Measuring success**: Evaluating the performance of personalized and adaptive prompts can be challenging, as success may vary from user to user. It's essential to develop proper evaluation metrics and gather user feedback to ensure that the prompts are indeed improving user satisfaction and achieving desired results.

4. **Bias and fairness**: Ensuring that personalized and adaptive prompts do not exacerbate existing biases or create unfair situations for certain user groups is essential. This can be achieved by employing fairness-aware machine learning techniques and continually monitoring prompt performance across diverse user groups.

When it comes to developing personalized and adaptive prompts, it is important to keep a few key challenges and considerations in mind. For instance, one challenge is ensuring that the prompts are actually personalized and adaptive to each individual user, which can be a complex task. Additionally, it is important to consider how the prompts will be received and perceived by users, as well as any potential drawbacks that may come with this approach.

However, if these challenges and considerations are carefully navigated, personalized and adaptive prompts can offer a range of benefits. These benefits may include increased engagement, improved learning outcomes, and a more effective overall learning experience. So, while the development of personalized and adaptive prompts may require some extra care and attention, the potential benefits make it a strategy that is well worth considering.

Chapter 9.3: Interdisciplinary Approaches

Prompt engineering can greatly benefit from interdisciplinary approaches. In this field, it is not enough to focus solely on computer science and AI. Instead, it is crucial to consider a multitude of factors that extend beyond these disciplines.

By combining insights from various fields such as linguistics, cognitive science, psychology, and sociology, prompt engineers can develop a more nuanced understanding of user behavior and preferences.

This can help them create more effective, nuanced, and human-centered prompts that cater to diverse user needs. Moreover, by engaging with a wide range of disciplines, prompt engineers can stay up-to-date with the latest research and trends, enabling them to stay ahead of the curve in this rapidly evolving field.

In this section, we will explore some examples of interdisciplinary approaches to prompt engineering and discuss the advantages of integrating knowledge from multiple fields.

Examples:

1. **Linguistics**: Linguistic theory and natural language processing techniques can help engineers understand the structure and nuances of human language, allowing them to design prompts that communicate more effectively with users. For instance, understanding the principles of syntax, semantics, and pragmatics can help create clearer and more contextually appropriate prompts.
2. **Cognitive Science**: Insights from cognitive science can help engineers design prompts that align with human cognitive processes, such as memory, attention, and problem-solving. By understanding the cognitive load and mental models of users, engineers can develop prompts that simplify complex tasks and improve user experience.
3. **Psychology**: Psychological principles can be applied to prompt engineering to influence user behavior and emotions. Techniques from behavioral psychology, such as reinforcement learning and nudge theory, can be employed to create prompts that encourage desired actions and discourage undesirable ones. Additionally, understanding user emotions and personality traits can help tailor prompts for different user types.
4. **Sociology**: Considering social and cultural factors in prompt engineering can lead to more inclusive and context-sensitive prompts. By understanding the social norms, values, and

expectations of diverse user groups, engineers can create prompts that resonate with users and avoid potential misunderstandings or cultural insensitivity.

5. **Ethics**: As AI systems become increasingly prevalent in society, it is crucial to incorporate ethical considerations into prompt engineering. Engineers must ensure that their prompts do not propagate harmful biases, discriminate against certain user groups, or infringe on user privacy.

By embracing interdisciplinary approaches, prompt engineers can create more sophisticated, effective, and human-centered AI systems that cater to the diverse needs and expectations of users. This holistic perspective not only improves the overall user experience but also fosters trust and long-term engagement with AI technologies. For instance, an interdisciplinary team of engineers, social scientists, and designers can work together to identify potential ethical issues and biases in AI systems early on and mitigate them before they cause harm.

Additionally, taking a human-centered approach means involving users in the design process and soliciting their feedback throughout the development cycle, which leads to more user-friendly and useful AI systems.

Ultimately, by prioritizing interdisciplinarity and human-centered design, prompt engineers can create AI systems that not only meet the functional requirements but also enhance the quality of life and well-being of users.

9.4: Legal and Regulatory Developments

As AI technologies, including prompt engineering, become more widespread, governments and regulatory bodies worldwide are developing legal frameworks and guidelines to address the challenges and potential risks associated with their use. In this section, we will explore the key legal and regulatory developments that impact prompt engineering.

9.4.1 Data Protection and Privacy

The General Data Protection Regulation (GDPR) in the European Union and the California Consumer Privacy Act (CCPA) in the United States are examples of data protection and privacy regulations that have implications for prompt engineering. These regulations govern how personal data is collected, stored, and processed, requiring AI practitioners to consider the privacy implications of their work and implement necessary safeguards to protect user data.

9.4.2 AI Ethics Guidelines

Various organizations and governmental bodies have issued AI ethics guidelines to promote the responsible development and use of AI technologies. For instance, the European Commission's High-Level Expert Group on AI released guidelines centered around seven key requirements for trustworthy AI, including transparency, accountability, and fairness. While not legally binding, these guidelines help inform the development of AI systems, including prompt engineering, and encourage the adoption of ethical best practices.

9.4.3 Algorithmic Transparency and Accountability

As AI systems increasingly influence decision-making processes, there is a growing demand for algorithmic transparency and accountability. Regulations such as the Algorithmic Accountability Act in the United States propose requiring organizations to conduct impact assessments of their AI systems to evaluate their potential risks and biases. This would directly impact prompt engineering, as developers would need to evaluate their prompt designs and implementations to ensure compliance with such regulations.

9.4.4 Intellectual Property Rights

AI-generated content has raised questions around intellectual property rights and ownership. For example, the United States Patent and Trademark Office (USPTO) is exploring the implications of AI-generated content for copyright and patent law. AI practitioners in the field of prompt engineering should be aware of these ongoing discussions and potential changes in intellectual property regulations.

9.4.5 International Cooperation and Harmonization

As AI technologies continue to evolve, there is a need for international cooperation and harmonization of legal and regulatory frameworks. Organizations like the International Telecommunication Union (ITU) and the Organization for Economic Co-operation and Development (OECD) are working to develop global AI policy standards and guidelines to ensure a more unified approach to AI regulation across different countries.

9.4.6 Cross-border Data Flows

As AI systems increasingly rely on data from multiple countries, navigating cross-border data flow regulations will become crucial. Ensuring compliance with data transfer mechanisms, such as the EU-US Privacy Shield, can impact how AI practitioners in prompt engineering design and implement their systems.

9.4.7 Sector-Specific Regulations

Certain industries, such as healthcare or finance, have specific regulations governing the use of AI. For instance, in healthcare, the Health Insurance Portability and Accountability Act (HIPAA) in the United States dictates the handling of protected health information. Prompt engineering practitioners working in these sectors should be aware of the industry-specific rules and regulations.

9.4.8 Evolving Standards and Best Practices

As the AI field matures, new standards and best practices will emerge to address the challenges and risks associated with AI technologies. Following organizations and initiatives focused on AI ethics and safety, like OpenAI or the Partnership on AI, can help prompt engineering practitioners stay up-to-date on the latest developments and adapt their practices accordingly.

In summary, the field of AI is undergoing rapid legal and regulatory changes, and it is crucial for engineering practitioners to stay informed and adapt to these changes. With the emergence of new technologies, the legal framework is struggling to keep up with the pace of innovation. As a result, the legal and regulatory landscape surrounding AI is constantly evolving. It is essential for engineering practitioners to be aware of these changes and to comply with relevant laws and regulations in order to ensure the responsible development and deployment of AI technologies.

One of the most important aspects of responsible AI development is ensuring that AI systems are transparent and explainable. This means that stakeholders should be able to understand how the AI system works and how it arrives at its decisions. This is particularly important in industries where AI systems make critical decisions that can have significant ramifications. For example, in the healthcare industry, AI systems are being used to help diagnose diseases and develop treatment plans. In these cases, it is essential for the AI system to be explainable so that healthcare practitioners can understand how the system arrived at its diagnosis and treatment recommendations.

Another important aspect of responsible AI development is ensuring that AI systems are fair and unbiased. This is particularly important in industries where AI systems are used to make decisions that impact people's lives, such as hiring decisions or loan approvals. There is a risk that AI systems can perpetuate and even amplify existing biases in society. Therefore, it is important for engineering practitioners to be aware of these risks and to take steps to mitigate them.

In conclusion, responsible AI development and deployment requires engineering practitioners to stay informed about legal and regulatory developments and to ensure that AI systems are transparent, explainable, fair, and unbiased. By doing so, we can ensure that AI technologies are developed and deployed in a responsible and ethical manner, and that they benefit society as a whole.

CHAPTER 10: Conclusion

10.1: Key Takeaways

As we conclude this book, let's revisit the key takeaways in the field of prompt engineering and AI language models:

1. **Importance of Prompt Engineering**: The book has demonstrated the critical role of prompt engineering in maximizing the performance and utility of AI language models like GPT-4. By crafting effective prompts, practitioners can harness the full potential of these powerful tools.
2. **Foundations of Prompt Engineering**: Understanding the basics of prompt engineering, including the components of prompts, techniques for crafting them, and strategies for evaluating their effectiveness, is essential for successful AI applications.
3. **Advanced Strategies and Techniques**: We explored advanced prompt engineering strategies, such as adversarial prompts, compositional prompts, and reinforcement learning, to further refine and optimize AI language model outputs.
4. **Real-World Applications**: The book showcased numerous real-world applications of prompt engineering across various domains, including content generation, question answering, language translation, and sentiment analysis, demonstrating the versatility and value of this skill.
5. **Ethical Considerations**: The book emphasized the importance of addressing bias and discrimination, ensuring privacy and data protection, and fostering transparency and

accountability in prompt engineering and AI system deployment.

6. **Future Trends and Challenges**: The book explored emerging trends, such as interdisciplinary approaches, personalization, adaptive prompts, and legal and regulatory developments, which will shape the future landscape of prompt engineering and AI.

As AI language models continue to advance, the art and science of prompt engineering will become increasingly important. With new applications and use cases emerging every day, it is essential for practitioners to stay up-to-date with the latest techniques and strategies.

In order to be effective, AI solutions must not only be accurate, but also ethical and impactful. This requires a deep understanding of the nuances and complexities of language, as well as a commitment to responsible development and deployment.

Fortunately, this book provides a comprehensive guide to the best practices and principles of prompt engineering. By following these guidelines, practitioners can ensure that their AI solutions are not only effective, but also aligned with their values and goals.

In addition to covering the technical aspects of prompt engineering, the book also explores the broader implications and applications of AI. From healthcare to finance, education to entertainment, AI has the potential to revolutionize every aspect of society. By mastering the techniques and strategies presented in this book, practitioners can contribute to creating a better, more equitable future for all.

10.2: Continuing Your Prompt Engineering Journey

As you conclude this book and look forward to further developing your skills in prompt engineering, it's essential to embrace continuous learning and stay informed about the latest advancements in the field. The landscape of AI and language models is constantly changing, and your growth as a prompt engineer depends on your ability to adapt to these changes. Here are some suggestions to help you continue your prompt engineering journey:

1. **Keep up to date**: At Cuantum Technologies, we are constantly creating new books with the latest information and innovations. Stay tuned by checking our book website section at books.cuantum.tech to learn about the most recent books on AI technologies, programming, and computer sciences.
2. **Engage with the AI community**: Participate in online forums, attend conferences, and join local AI and machine learning groups to network with other professionals and stay informed about the latest research and developments.
3. **Collaborate on projects**: Work on real-world projects with other AI practitioners to gain practical experience in prompt engineering. This hands-on experience will help solidify the concepts you've learned and expose you to new challenges and techniques.
4. **Stay updated with research**: Regularly read AI research papers and follow leading AI researchers and organizations on social media platforms. Keeping up with the latest research will help you stay at the cutting edge of prompt engineering and AI technologies.
5. **Learn from online resources**: Take advantage of online courses, tutorials, and blog posts to deepen your understanding of prompt engineering and related topics. Many experts in the field share their insights and knowledge through these platforms, providing valuable learning opportunities.
6. **Experiment and iterate**: As a prompt engineer, it's crucial to keep experimenting with different techniques and strategies to improve your prompt design skills. Continuously iterate on your prompts, evaluate their performance, and refine them to better suit your specific use cases.

By following these recommendations and maintaining a growth mindset, you'll be well-equipped to navigate the ever-evolving world of prompt engineering and AI. It's important to remember that prompt engineering is a field that is constantly changing, with new developments and techniques emerging all the time. With this in mind, it's essential to stay curious and continue learning, so that you can keep up with the latest trends and developments in the field.

In addition to staying curious and continuing to learn, it's also important to embrace the challenges that come your way as you further your prompt engineering journey. Whether you're faced with a difficult problem to solve, a new tool or technology to learn, or a challenging project to complete, remember that these challenges are opportunities for growth and development. By approaching these challenges with a growth mindset, you'll be able to overcome them and emerge stronger and more skilled than before.

So, as you navigate the world of prompt engineering and AI, remember to stay curious, continue learning, and embrace the challenges that come your way. By doing so, you'll be well on your way to success in this exciting and dynamic field.

10.3: The Future of AI and Human Collaboration

As we look towards the future, the role of AI in human collaboration will continue to grow and evolve. Prompt engineering is just one facet of this expanding partnership between humans and machines. The potential for AI to enhance human capabilities, improve decision-making, and foster innovation is immense. In this closing topic, let's explore some examples and predictions of how AI and human collaboration might develop in the future:

1. **Augmented decision-making**: AI systems, like advanced language models, will increasingly provide decision-makers with valuable insights and perspectives to inform their choices. By leveraging AI, humans can uncover patterns and trends that would be difficult or impossible to detect otherwise, leading to more informed and effective decision-making.
2. **Creative collaboration**: AI has the potential to augment human creativity by generating new ideas, concepts, and designs. In areas such as art, music, and literature, AI can act

as a creative partner, offering inspiration and assisting in the development of innovative works.

3. **Enhanced communication**: As AI-powered language models improve, they will facilitate more effective communication between individuals, teams, and even across languages. AI can help bridge language barriers, making global collaboration easier and more efficient.

4. **AI-assisted education and training**: AI will play a pivotal role in personalized learning experiences, adapting educational content to suit individual learners' needs and preferences. AI can also assist in training professionals, providing targeted guidance and support based on their specific learning goals.

5. **Ethical AI systems**: As AI technologies advance, so too will the focus on ethical considerations. We can expect to see increased efforts to develop AI systems that are fair, transparent, and accountable, ensuring that they respect human values and operate within ethical boundaries.

6. **Human-AI teaming**: In various industries, human-AI teams will become more commonplace as AI systems complement and enhance human capabilities. From healthcare to finance, these collaborations will lead to better outcomes and drive innovation.

In conclusion, it is clear that AI and human collaboration is an area with tremendous potential for growth and development. The advancing technologies surrounding AI are becoming more and more integrated into our daily lives, opening up new opportunities for positive impact. One example of this is prompt engineering, which demonstrates how AI can be used to empower humans and help them achieve their goals.

Looking ahead, it is clear that there is still so much to explore when it comes to human-AI collaboration, and that this exploration will lead to unprecedented growth and progress in the years to come. As we continue to delve further into this exciting field, we can only imagine what the future holds and what new possibilities will arise as a result of the combined strengths of both humans and AI.

Conclusion

As we reach the end of this comprehensive guide on prompt engineering, we, at Cuantum Technologies, want to reflect on the incredible journey we have taken together. We have delved deep into the intricacies of prompt engineering, exploring its foundations, techniques, applications, and ethical considerations. We have also looked ahead to the emerging trends and challenges that prompt engineering and the broader field of AI will face in the coming years. In this conclusion, we will recap the key takeaways from each chapter and underscore the importance of continuing your prompt engineering journey in a world where AI is becoming increasingly integral to our lives.

In the first chapter, we introduced the concept of prompt engineering and highlighted its significance in harnessing the full potential of AI-powered language models like OpenAI's GPT series. We discussed the limitations of these models and emphasized the need for skilled prompt engineers to optimize and control their outputs.

The second chapter focused on understanding AI language models and their underlying mechanisms. We examined the architecture of transformer models and the training process they undergo, including pre-training and fine-tuning. This knowledge is essential for prompt engineers to grasp the capabilities and limitations of the models they work with.

In the third chapter, we covered the fundamentals of prompt engineering. We discussed various techniques, including refining prompts, controlling verbosity, and temperature tuning, that allow prompt engineers to guide AI language models effectively. By mastering these techniques, you can ensure more accurate and useful outputs from the AI models you work with.

The fourth chapter delved into the art and science of designing effective prompts. We explored strategies for composing prompts that elicit the desired responses from AI models, with an emphasis on iterative prompt design and the importance of experimentation.

In chapter five, we took a closer look at the iterative prompt design process. We discussed the importance of iteration and feedback loops in refining prompts, and we emphasized the value of A/B testing, collaboration, and the use of external data sources in this process.

Chapter six introduced advanced prompt engineering strategies, such as chaining and nesting prompts, which enable prompt engineers to tackle more complex tasks and achieve better outcomes. We also covered prompt engineering for non-English languages and the challenges associated with multilingual AI models.

In the seventh chapter, we showcased real-world applications and use cases of prompt engineering, ranging from content generation and editing to sentiment analysis and text classification. These examples illustrated the versatility of prompt engineering and the myriad ways it can be applied to solve real-world problems.

Chapter eight addressed the ethical considerations in prompt engineering, such as addressing bias and discrimination, privacy and data protection, transparency, and accountability. We emphasized the importance of developing AI systems that are fair, transparent, and respect human values.

In the penultimate chapter, we discussed future trends and challenges in prompt engineering, including emerging AI architectures, personalization, interdisciplinary approaches, and legal and regulatory developments. We highlighted the importance of keeping up with these trends and adapting to the ever-evolving landscape of AI technology.

Finally, in the tenth chapter, we distilled the key takeaways from the book, encouraged you to continue your prompt engineering journey, and contemplated the future of AI and human collaboration. We explored the myriad ways AI can empower humans and foster innovation, and how prompt engineering is just one example of how AI and humans can work together to drive progress.

As a software development company specializing in AI, Cuantum Technologies is deeply invested in the advancement and responsible deployment of AI technologies. We believe that prompt engineering holds great promise for improving the utility and safety of AI language models and unlocking their full potential. Our goal in writing this book was to provide you with the knowledge, tools, and inspiration to embark on your own prompt engineering journey and contribute to the development of AI systems that empower humans and drive innovation.

In the ever-evolving landscape of AI, staying current with new developments and adapting to emerging trends is essential. As a prompt engineer, you will need to continually refine your skills and expand your knowledge to stay at the forefront of this rapidly changing field. We encourage you to participate in online forums, attend conferences, and collaborate with other professionals to share insights and learn from one another.

As AI language models continue to advance, becoming more powerful and capable, it is crucial to develop and maintain a strong ethical foundation. By prioritizing fairness, transparency, and respect for human values, you can ensure that your work contributes to the responsible growth of AI technology.

Moreover, the interdisciplinary nature of AI and prompt engineering means that there is much to gain from exploring other fields, such as cognitive science, linguistics, and psychology. By fostering a deep understanding of the underlying principles governing human language and cognition, you can better inform your prompt engineering strategies and develop more effective AI systems.

Finally, we believe that the future of AI lies in the symbiosis of human and machine intelligence. By leveraging the power of AI and the creativity of human minds, we can unlock unprecedented opportunities for innovation and progress. Prompt engineering is just one example of how AI and humans can collaborate to solve complex problems and create a brighter future.

In conclusion, we hope this book has provided you with valuable insights and practical guidance on your prompt engineering journey. By mastering the techniques and strategies outlined in these pages, you can play a pivotal role in shaping the future of AI-powered language models and unlocking their full potential. As you continue to explore the world of prompt engineering, we wish you the best of luck and look forward to witnessing the incredible innovations that arise from the collaboration between humans and AI.

Cuantum Technologies

Know more about us

At Cuantum Technologies, we specialize in building web applications that deliver creative experiences and solve real-world problems. Our developers have expertise in a wide range of programming languages and frameworks, including Python, Django, React, Three,js, and Vue.js, among others. We are constantly exploring new technologies and techniques to stay at the forefront of the industry, and we pride ourselves on our ability to create solutions that meet our clients' needs.

If you are interested in learning more about our Cuantum Technologies and the services that we offer, please visit our website at books.cuantum.tech. We would be happy to answer any questions that you may have and to discuss how we can help you with your software development needs.

www.cuantum.tech

Made in the USA
Coppell, TX
09 November 2023

24017719R00085